PENGUIN BOOKS

THE COUNTRYSIDE EX

John Seymour was born in 1914 and, as he puts it, 'mis-educated in England and Switzerland'. After studying at an agricultural college, he worked on farms in England for two years and then spent some ten years in Africa where, among other things, he managed a sheep and cattle farm and acted as livestock officer for a government veterinary department. During the war he served with the King's African Rifles, first in Ethiopia and then in Burma; and afterwards travelled widely in India, Ceylon and the Middle East.

He and his wife Sally returned to England in 1956 and settled down to running a five-acre small-holding in Suffolk. Then, in 1964, the Seymours moved to Pembrokeshire and a sixty-two-acre farm called Fachongle Isaf, which had been empty a year and was producing nothing but thistle seeds. In the years since, Fachongle Isaf has been transformed, and is now run as a cooperative, producing every crop it is possible to grow in West Wales, as well as husbanding cows, sheep, pigs, bees, chickens, geese and ducks.

John Seymour has lived a life of almost total self-sufficiency for more than twenty years and is the acknowledged authority on the subject. His experience has been distilled in three practical guides: *Self-Sufficiency* (with Sally Seymour, 1973), *The Complete Book of Self-Sufficiency* (1976), and *The Self-Sufficient Gardener* (1978). In addition, Mr Seymour has written *Fat of the Land* (1961), *I'm a Stranger Here Myself* (1978) and *Gardener's Delight* (1978).

JOHN SEYMOUR

THE COUNTRYSIDE EXPLAINED

*

with illustrations by
Sally Seymour

PENGUIN BOOKS

Penguin Books Ltd, Harmondsworth, Middlesex, England
Penguin Books, 625 Madison Avenue, New York, New York 10022, U.S.A.
Penguin Books Australia Ltd, Ringwood, Victoria, Australia
Penguin Books Canada Ltd, 2801 John Street, Markham, Ontario, Canada L3R 1B4
Penguin Books (N.Z.) Ltd, 182–190 Wairau Road, Auckland 10, New Zealand

—

First published by Faber and Faber 1977
Published in Penguin Books 1979

—

Copyright © John Seymour, 1977
All rights reserved

—

Made and printed in Great Britain by
Richard Clay (The Chaucer Press) Ltd,
Bungay, Suffolk

Its plains are spacious, its hills are pleasantly situated, adapted to superior tillage, and its mountains admirably calculated for the alternative pasturage of cattle, where flowers of various colours, trodden by the feet of man, give it the appearance of a lovely picture. It is decked, like a man's chosen bride, with divers jewels, with lucid fountains and abundant brooks wandering over its snow-white sands; with transparent rivers flowing in gentle murmurs and offering a sweet pledge of repose to those who recline upon their banks, whilst it is watered by abundant lakes which issue forth cool torrents.

England, as described by the monk Gildas, circa A.D. 550

Contents

Chapter 1

The People of the Countryside

'The best crop any land can raise is a happy, healthy people.'
                              Mary French, *The Worm in the Wheat*

To the superficial observer from the towns it may seem as though the people of the countryside are exactly the same as the ones he left behind him in the city. They dress the same, look the same, live in the same sort of houses with the same sort of china ducks in flight across the wall, eat the same sort of food and also listen to *The Archers*. A farmer who grows a thousand acres of wheat has his wrapped sliced loaf delivered at his door like everybody else. A farmer who milks a hundred cows twice a day buys his butter. Farm workers no longer look weatherbeaten because they spend all their working lives in the cabs of tractors (cabs are now obligatory on all tractors driven by employed men). Local accents and dialects have been ironed out by education and television. If you meet a farmer, or farm worker, or anybody else connected with the land, when he is away from his job, there is absolutely no way of telling him from a city man.

There has been considerable pressure in the last thirty or forty years to bring this state of affairs about; for various factors combined to make the countryman feel inferior to the townsman. The latter had much higher wages, much shorter hours, worked in the warm and dry, wore smart clothes, had an apparent sophistication and was in touch with the great world. The qualities that the countryman had—toughness and hardiness, sharp intelligence uneroded by a constant stream of trivial information, native wit, deep

11

understanding of the universe as it really is around us—these things became undervalued and decried. Nowadays a meeting of a branch of the National Farmers Union is indistinguishable from a convention of bank managers.

It was not always so. Well after the Second World War I used to go every Tuesday, which was market day, to the Farmers' Ordinary Luncheon at the Golden Lion in Ipswich. We all sat at a long table and the main dish was generally silverside of beef—and very good it was too. The men I ate with really looked like farmers: they dressed like farmers—several of them even going to the length of knee-breeches and canvas leggings or 'elijas' as we called them in Suffolk. They gloried in talking the drawling, broad Suffolk dialect. Their wit was sharp and quick and you had to be quick too, and very much with it, to understand it.

But meanwhile, if we wish to discover what the countryman was like before he made himself indistinguishable from the townsman (and I believe this difference is actually only very superficial), we must seek out country people and ask them how it was in their early days. To do this very thing I travelled in 1960 over much of England and Wales looking for articulate old men and women, to record their memories on tape. I came quickly to realize that the gulf which yawned between them and their children's generation was greater perhaps than that which lay between any two generations in the history of the world. I felt as though I was diving back into a pre-industrial past: an era which was far closer to the Elizabethan age than to ours.

'It was different altogether in them days. You lived *in* you see. Lived in on the farm. Four of us there when I started on the farm. We were as happy as could be! We'd get up in the morning—four or five o'clock—depended how far we had to fetch the horses in summer time. Sometimes they'd run about! It was a job to get 'em in. But we'd got to be in to our breakfast at twenty to six and out from there at six—and out from the stable at half past. 'Twas nice work. Following the plough—whistling and singing all day . . . [and he sang]:

> When six o'clock comes to breakfast we meet
> With bread beef and pork boys we heartily eat

With a piece in our pocket I'll swear and I'll vow
That we're all jolly fellows that follow the plough!

And off to our ploughing each good fellow goes
We trip oe'r the plains as nimbly as does
And when we get there so jolly and bold
To see which of us the straight furrow can hold. . . .

Those were the exact words of Lane the Drum, as I recorded them, sitting in the flower-hung porch of his little cottage behind Wenlock Edge in Shropshire, sipping his excellent parsley wine.

scythe

I had been driving along this remote lane one flaming day in June, and had seen an old man scything grass on a very steep hillside. I stopped and climbed up to him. I had a strange sensation that he had been expecting me. 'I were just going to have a rest!' he said. 'Come down and have a drop of wine.'

Arthur Lane was his name, but they called him Lane the Drum because he lived in a house which had once been a pub called 'The Drum and Monkey'. He lived all alone, far from anybody, but still worked on a farm although he was over seventy.

He told me how his father had been a warrener and how, when he had left school at ten, he had helped him catch rabbits. 'Then as soon as I was fourteen there was a gentleman farmer wanted me—not far away—to see to his hackneys and to clean his boots. He said he'd give me five pounds—and me father said *he'd* give me five pounds for the twelve months if I'd stay with him. I was getting a little bit useful. But I preferred the horses so I went with him. I got five pounds the first year then he got me to stop again—seven pounds the next year—then he wanted me to stop again but—no—he'd offended me a bit so I left.

'I went with cart-horses the next year—I got nine pounds. Then I left again at May—I was sixteen then and I thought I ought to be worth more . . .' and he worked himself up from his first five pounds a year until he was living in the farmhouse and getting twenty-four pounds a year. 'Never broke a year though, nor never drawed any money during the twelve months. I'd saved enough from the rabbitting to get my clothes and that like. If I got sent to market the master'd give me a shilling to buy some bread and cheese and baccy with.'

He moved to a larger farm. 'We all lived in—nine of us. Oh it was grand fun! Butcher used to bring us a lump of beef to last us a week, and it was boiled in the furnace on the Sunday, and then a girl used to go on the Monday morning with a three-legged iron pot, ladle this pot full of broth out of the furnace and boil it—and we used to have to bread our own basins—ladle our broth—and there was some of the beef on the table as well—*and* cheese—*good* living! *And* beer! Home-brewed beer. Used to brew twice a year—March and October—didn't have any tea. Not the two years I was there. *Good* living! *Good* living!'

In the evening, in the hot summer time: 'We would take the horses in and give them some hay, then we'd go into the house and have our supper, then we'd take the horses out into the field after—up into the hollow there—*nice* and warm—in the start *talk*—then one'd get down on his knees, talking, then he'd sit down—then another'd get down—and *another*'d get down, quietly like, *and we have gone to sleep there*. And slept the night.'

When a man married he moved out of the big farmhouse, of course, and had a tied cottage of his own.

'In the hay harvest the married men had a pound, whether it lasted a fortnight or three weeks or a month. See they worked when they could at the hay harvest—wet nights they'd go home after six o'clock at night. And the corn harvest—they had a month. That was from six in the morning to eight at night whatever the weather was—if they couldn't harvest they'd go hedge-brushing or go spreading manure. The married men had two pounds for that—and us single men worked the same time and we never had anything! It didn't seem fair to me—and it doesn't now! I often think of that!' And the little old man laughed merrily. If an injustice wasn't good for anything else it was good enough to laugh at.

'In the winter we'd have to thresh—in the barn. Flail-threshing when I started. I remember when I first tried to use it—long and short stick you know. I swung the flail and hit meself on the back of the head!'

Then came the horse-driven threshing machine—the jin-ring outside the barn around which a horse walked in a circle to drive a threshing machine within. Then, on a windy day, they'd winnow. Open the two great doors opposite each other (that is why an old barn is built like a church—with two transepts) and toss the threshed corn up into the air with shovels so that the chaff would blow away.

'Then I got married!' And he laughed again.

He left his job, bought two horses and a big spring brake, and set up in the carrier's trade. He did well, but the First World War started and put an end to it. Then he took a pub, 'The Drum and Monkey', and did very well but he lost his licence. So he started a smallholding on eight acres. It is generally accepted nowadays that a farmer cannot make a living on less than three hundred.

'Bought three bullocks to fatten. Seven pounds each! Now they'd be fifty pounds—difference in the times. Different feeding too—in them days meat more firmer. Sheep too—out on swedes. Feel 'em—*firm* meat—more substantial. Meat now got nothing in it.'

Then he had a run of bad luck—'enough to make a man give up.

The first three years I did very well. Then I lost my wife. Then I lost a mare and her foal—well, the foal first and then the mare. I lost a heifer and calf. And then I lost a gilt and eleven pigs. All in three months and nothing'd stop it! People said "I should think you'll give up!" "Not I!" I said. "My life's before me."'

He took a job with the council, tarring the roads, and went on running his smallholding at the same time. 'Got up at four—feed the animals—there by seven o'clock in the morning, when it was fine stop there 'til seven o'clock at night—bike there and back—seventeen or eighteen miles. Feed me pigs, have me dinner; then I'd got some land two miles away—bike up there. Then I'd got some a mile further—on the top. Be half-past eleven or twelve o'clock when I'd get home here. Then I'd have a lump of bread and cheese—cup of tea, coffee or cocoa or something and be off to bed and it'd be a quarter past twelve. Then four hours in bed and off and up again. Stick it? Stuck it well! People used to tell me and say: "It'll make an old man of you!" It never hurt me! [Mr Lane is now eighty—and still runs his smallholding and remains one of the fittest and liveliest old men I have ever seen.] Work be never hard—it's only hard if you *take* it hard. I was determined. And I got going again. Then I got overstocked. Had to get more land. Left the council and started full time farming.'

I saw a beat-up melodeon hanging on the wall. Mr Lane got it down and struck up a country song. 'Oh, I used to like to sing and play, days gone by. They always wanted me to go down to the pub— sing and play to 'em. Don't go there much now though. But I still love a song.'

I asked him how he thought we modern men compared with the men of his day.

'Well, there's not the strong men about as used to be. Or they don't try—I don't know which it is. Well, the weight of a bag of beans was fourteen score five, wheat twelve score, barley eleven score four. I could carry anything—well I never tried anything more. Three hundredweight—could carry it up a ladder or up the granary steps.' He is a small man.

'How did you amuse yourselves?'

'Oh, we made our own amusements! In the winter evenings we used to sing, you know. Each take a turn to sing a song and the farmer's wife and daughter'd play the harmonica. And gymnastics. We were up to all sorts in them days. Used to do gymnastics in the cowsheds, we young men. Climb up on the rafters and turn somersaults. Rope-climbing—boxing—wrestling. Lift these old fifty-sixes. Oh—long ladder across the beams and just jump up and catch that with your hands. Walking the rungs—beat one another on that—see who could go the farthest. Rope tied across the building—get across that. And of course I used to be there with the melodeon—somebody stepping. Oh I could do some of that now!' and he did a step-dance for me. 'Yes—lie down in the straw after we'd finished the horses at night and we'd sing to twelve o'clock, very often, in the winter time.'

'Are you afraid of death?' I asked.

'Death?' He laughed and his eyes twinkled. 'Death? *No!* I don't intend to die yet awhile! And when I do it's nothing to be feared of. I'll take it as it comes.' Lane the Drum had rigged and victualled his ship of death.

Mr Lane was one of many men that I interviewed who had started working life living in on a big farm. Here is Mr Hancock, retired farm labourer, who lives in the Golden Valley in Herefordshire:

'Five bob a week—and live in and you were on from six o'clock in the morning until maybe nine at night—according—like in the summer, you see. You lived in the farm, when you started, about fifteen, you'd draw your money if you wanted a sub, then you'd go on for twelve months—you knew you wouldn't be going to town, only perhaps to go to market to drive stock or something you see—

17

well, they might give you a bob to go and have your dinner, you see—well, you'd have a dinner for about ninepence—a *good* dinner, see. Now once you've finished working for the day all you've got to do is settle in, see. You couldn't go out to no recreation like you can now, see. You was just—well, in a way I think you was more happier then than what you be now. . . .'

As for the women—here is Mrs Edith Turner, also in the Golden Valley, very old when I met her, living in a small, very narrow cottage the walls of which were so covered with decorative objects inside that there was hardly room for a fly to light between them. Framed photographs of relatives, polished brass-work, lace plates, Victorial oleographs—not an inch to spare, and a nice big flitch of salt bacon hung up in a corner. She is a small, thin, happy woman, and her lovely Herefordshire accent seemed very Welsh to me when I first heard it—now I live in Wales it sounds English.

'My father was a smallholder and butcher. Food? Well, we had plenty. Well, we had home-made butter, home-made cheese, home-made jam—nothing bought—you know—all our own. Home-cured bacon—all our own pigs was cured and all. And I think we was far better off than we are now—in the shape of food. It was good—it was really. But of course—we hadn't got the *money* to spend. I had about threepence a year to spend on sweets!' (But at eighty she still had her own teeth!)

'Say we'd do the washing on Monday, Tuesday we may do butter and Wednesday we'd go to market—Hereford was the market around here. Thursday we'd do the cheese, baking on the Friday—of course, between these things we'd do all the other work of the house, you see. Bread we used to do in the bread oven—heat the oven first with wood—get it so hot—you'd get to know all that—had to do all that you see—used to use either oak or ash to heat the oven—cordwood sticks we used to call that years ago. We used to make it—a big bath or steen—one of those pans you know which we call steens. Well then you put your flour in, so much, so much yeast, mix it up and put it in there and leave it to rise then for a couple of hours—'til it did rise up—you could see it rising. Get your oven hot while it was doing—to heat—and then you'd knead it up like, into loaves—cottage loaves as a rule—clean your oven out when it got hot like—

and then put the dough in the oven—shut it up—seal it.' (I must explain that the fire was actually lit *in* the oven. When it was hot the ashes were drawn and the bread put in.) 'It was our own wheat and our own flour and it was good—you couldn't beat it.

'We killed our own pigs and made our own bacon. It did keep all the year round, pretty well. Nothing better than home-cured ham and bacon. Look—I still use it—look I have a side hung up there! Shop bacon isn't cured enough and it won't keep—and bacon has no taste to it if it isn't kept for a while. I soaks it overnight and either boils it or fries it.'

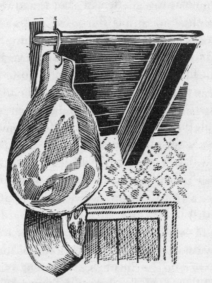

I asked her it if was not a lot of work.

'Work? Well no one had told us you see. No one had told us in them days that there was anything *wrong* with work. I liked work! I still do! There didn't seem to us to be anything wrong with work.'

But times changed for Edith—her father got ill. The doctor couldn't diagnose his illness. 'He did say: "Well I don't know what's the matter with you." "Well I don't if you don't," said my father. "Well it must be the tobacco," said the doctor. "You smoke too much tobacco." "Well do you think so?" said my father—"Well, I tell you what—I never smoked a cigarette or an ounce of tobacco in my life!"'

Edith's mother had to go out to work as cook in the workhouse. Edith told me how her father was hobbling by on two sticks one day while a 'roadster' (tramp) was sitting in the sunshine killing the lice which he was discovering in his shirt.

'Sorting 'em out then?' said Edith's father, cheerily.

'No, I'm not sorting them out,' said the tramp. 'I'm taking them as they come.'

Edith had to go out to work too, for without her father's labour the smallholding would not support them all. One felt that Edith's really happy days were over, although she still had spirit.

'I went from home to a gentleman's house and worked my way up to cook. My highest wage was thirty-five pounds a year. We had eight maids in the house and there were twenty-five men outside. They used to keep the race horses and small farm and all that. Oh I was often up at five in the morning—didn't go to bed 'til half past ten or eleven. On all day. I used to feather all the poultry and skin all the rabbits—there was plenty to do. Feed the dogs and all—keepers' dogs and all that. But we did have our bit of fun sometimes—it wasn't *too* bad. Oh—we'd get into a row sometimes—I can tell you!'

When Cobbett and Arthur Young were writing about farming people in the early part of the nineteenth century they both realized that the farm labourer had been well fed, adequately sheltered and well clad, but that he was even then falling on hard times. The *bull-frogs*, as Cobbett called the big commercial farmers of his day, were finding that labour was a buyer's market and all they had to give a man to get him to work for them was just enough to keep him alive. At that time too the cottager's common grazing was being taken away from him so that he could no longer keep a cow and some geese, and collect firewood and acorns for his pig. Farm workers' wages remained low after this, and are low now, and men like Arthur Lane and Mr Hancock were lucky to have worked for good farmers who ran prosperous farms. They may have been paid practically no money but they were well fed. Mr Garnett Keyte of Chipping Campden saw the more impoverished side of things. Chipping Campden was an old textile town, which had gone downhill as the mills all closed, and people there were very poor indeed. Garnett Keyte is a very prosperous market gardener, and a most expressive and articulate man.

His lovely Gloucestershire accent is a joy to listen to, but his story is sad.

'It was the time of Joe Archer, you know, when he organized the trade unions. But they was very poor—nine shillings a week—some of the men worked and brought up a family on it—nine shillings a week, mind you. Some of them had twelve shillings a week. And there were six days to the week and if the master wanted them on a Sunday they'd got to go. And they daren't say no—there was some-body else wanted the job, you know. They could buy tack cheap we know—but then where did nine shillings go? Some of them was that poor they had had their bread all on tick—all while the children were young, and then when they got a bit older and got a few shil-lings and went to work a bit, they went to Gavs and they said: "How much bread—have you kept count of it Mr Gavs?" And he said yes and they paid every penny of it—didn't owe the man a penny. *Every-one* was poor beyond a few top-notchers you know.

'I can tell you a tale of one old man in Campden—which is a most wonderful tale. He was sitting down—they was going to have a bit of bacon, and a few swedes and a bit of taters one day for dinner. And they saw the vicar coming, and our old Jack—he rammed his fork though the bacon and stuck it up under the table—see—so the vicar shouldn't see they had bacon for dinner, see—that was a most wonderful affair. So the vicar came in and said: "Well, I'm very sorry", he said, "to come in while you poor people are having your meal—er—is that all you've got—potatoes and swedes?" And old Jack had got the Bible out and he put him on the table and he hit him with his fist—*thump*. And he said: "That's my vittle and drink Vicar —that Bible!" And of course he jarred the fork out and the bacon fell on the floor!'

Right the other side of England, in the pheasant-rearing Sandling country of Suffolk, my old friend Fred Baldwin, a carrier by trade, took poverty in his stride, just as he always used to take everything else.

'People were poor, but nine out of ten had a pig in the sty. You know—people had enough money just to knock along—they used to scheme somehow or other—beg borrow or steal. Go to an old jumble sale and buy up a suit and if that was too big for 'em they took it in and if that was too small they let it out! That's how you went on that time o' day. Go to an old second-hand clothes shop—you could rig yourself out for work—*t'ain't* likely! This wasn't a *posh* nation then —like it is today. That wouldn't be so posh now—if that weren't for hire-purchasism!

'Poaching! That's how we lived. But 'course that time o' day the keepers about here all reared pheasants—well I mean they thought nothing of going here and shooting a thousand in a day and *then* there was plenty for everybody else. Real notorious poachers! I don't say the *natives* done it—nine out of ten of the natives worked on these estates—you see, well, they daren't do it. They soon got cleared out —lose their cottage and their job—cleared right out.' Fred, though, never worked on an estate, and always lived in his own house.

'This weren't a posh nation! They didn't take na bloody notice o' that! I've seen girls go to school with their mother's shoes on— mother's dresses on—hung round their ankles. We used to pay into what we called a clothing club—poor old Mary Markham's at Nacton —and they used to go to Brand's in Ipswich—and they used to get the goods—and o' course they used to go by carrier . . . about once a year after harvest they used to go and get the things. I know there used to be a lot go over look to Shotley and they used to get their boots made—poor old Jack Wright of Shotley "Boot"—he used to make boots—he used to make 'em by hand. They used to last a year without being soled. They were a pound a pair.'

'Did you enjoy life in those days, Fred? Did you have a good time?'

'I did! And I'm having one now. I remember once—I'd been to "The Shepherd and Dog" this night—all night—it was Saturday night—left there about half past ten—had all I could manage you know. It was a hot, beautiful night. I thought to myself—I'll go down Tankard Meadow—I reckon there'll be some camping out down there tonight. The first two I met—"Hullo," I said, "got na beer?" They said no—they said, "You want to go down there—they got some." Well they had a gallon. It was a moonlight night—beautiful night. I laid down beside this gallon of beer. Full you know. I could hear they were all asleep you know. There was an ol' boy next to me —he was deaf and dumb. Well—about four o'clock in the morning

22

they began to wake up you know. So I could hear 'em a'talking you know. And this ol' boy—this deaf and dumb boy—picked this here gallon jar up you know—I suppose he thought that were a bit *light*— he picked that up and shook it. Well he couldn't *hear* it whether there was any in it or not because he was deaf and dumb—but he thought that was light and he tried to see if that were a'swuggling in there—and there worn't any! When I'd finished I'd drunk the whul gallon. And I was drunk when I went there and I was drunk when they woke up!'

It might have been on that very night, in a different age from ours, that Arthur Lane the Drum took the horses out into the meadow with his companions—'. . . then one'd get down on his knees, talking, then he'd sit down—then another'd get down—and *another*'d get down, quietly like, and we have gone to sleep there!'

> Ill fares the land, to hastening ills a prey
> Where wealth accumulates and men decay
> Princes and lords may flourish or may fade
> A breath can make them, as a breath has made;
> But a bold peasantry, their country's pride
> When once destroyed can never be supplied.
>
> Oliver Goldsmith, *The Deserted Village*

Chapter 2

The Story of English Farming

Thus the old country people; we must come now to the present day. But to discuss farming, the main industry of the present-day country-side, we have got to look at its past, to see how it developed into the present.

The countryside is farming, and farming is the countryside. If you get in an aeroplane and fly over England you can very well see that this is so: below you is an apparently endless chequerboard of fields with hedges round them, or in the upland areas fields with stone walls round them, and you get a feeling of incredulity that the enormous labour of clearing all the fields from the forest, and putting those hedges and stone walls around them, could ever have been done at all. You also come to realize, as you make such a flight, what a *lot* of land there is, all good farmland, in a country such as England. True there are scars: the occasional small town or village, a quarry here or there, and sometimes a great cancerous spread of a conurbation; but over vast stretches you see nothing but green country.

Sometimes the farmland is broken by high and apparently barren hills, but these are not barren, and are farmland too. Then there are stands of forestry, but this too is farming. Whether you grow cabbages or conifers on the land it is still farming: growing something we need and then harvesting it. Therefore any description of the countryside must be primarily a discussion of the farming countryside. The proper study of mankind is man, and the influence of man is all-pervading in settled countries. The influence can be benign, or it can be evil. Man can be a husbandman—or a destroyer.

24

Historians speculate endlessly on how such things as the taming of animals and the growing of crops were first developed; but somewhere in the world, even now, you can find humans in every stage of development. Consider the Namibian Bushmen and their 'Bushman grain'. The Bushmen are Paleolithic people, and if we wish to know how Paleolithic people lived we should go to Namibia before we start scratching around nearer home, and it is probably because archaeologists have never done this that they have never stumbled on the way in which *grain* first came to be eaten. But archaeologists stick to archaeology and anthropologists look after the Bushmen.

There are certain kinds of ants all over the world which collect grass seeds. They store these in their nests in large quantities. The Bushmen (and I have seen them do it) raid these nests and steal the grass seed from the ants. They roast it on a hot stone and eat it. I would be willing to wager a large sum that this is how grain first got to be eaten. After this it does not take the postulation of a genius to believe that somebody accidentally left some of his store of grass seed about in a damp place for a few days and noticed that it sprouted. Then, if it lay on the soil and the birds didn't eat it, it pushed roots down into the soil and grew. Then, if you buried it a little, the birds couldn't eat it. Farming had begun.

Farming is supposed to have developed in Mesopotamia about 9000 B.C. and to have reached Britain somewhere around 3700 B.C., brought by the direct ancestors of people we still find here among us where I live in Wales: smallish, dark, black-haired, long-headed, fine-nosed, very good-looking people known to ethnologists as the Mediterranean type. They are poetical, mystical, musical, emotional —but that is beside the point. They were Stone Age people, but could fell trees with stone axes and dig ground with sharpened, fire-hardened digging sticks. You can still find people at this stage of culture in Africa and other countries today, although contact with Western culture has replaced most of the digging-sticks with iron hoes.

In any case, these Neolithic people (as we call them) brought a kind of improved grass called Einkorn from the Fertile Crescent with them, and this made a much more settled form of civilization possible for them, for they could stay in the same place (indeed had to) and could start each winter in the knowledge that they would probably see the spring.

They probably practised a system of agriculture still used in Central Africa, in the Northern jungles of Ceylon (where it is known as *chena* cultivation), and indeed in many other tropical countries today. That is, they would invade the forest, cut down trees but not stump them, burn the timber and slash, cultivate the ground between the stumps and plant their wheat or other crops. Because the land was sure to be free of the weeds of disturbed ground (what we call 'arable' weeds nowadays) they would have to do a minimum of hoeing; they would be cashing the credit of thousands of years of forest-growth in the form of humus-rich land, the ashes of their burnings would give them an immediate supply of available potash and they would have got very good crops indeed for five or ten years or more with a minimum of labour. After that time, though the seeds of 'arable' weeds would have invaded the clearing, the stored fertility would have been used up (they did not yet understand the *Law of Return* of the land—that you must put back what you take out) and so they would abandon that clearing and go and make another somewhere else. This sounds like terribly bad husbandry from a forester's point of view, but provided the population is small enough it is not as bad as it sounds. The forest rapidly regenerates itself: in thirty years a climax vegetation of high forest trees is again established and then it can be cleared again and the process repeated. Hundreds of people were starved to death in the northern jungle of Ceylon during the twenties and thirties of this century because doctrinaire forestry officers used police and troops to stop *chena* cultivation. Now the people are allowed to do it again and everything goes on perfectly well: there is plenty of jungle still in Northern Ceylon (nay, far too much, I used to think when I had to march about in it) and the *chena* cultivators do not starve to death. Incidentally just as the principle of *ley farming* (ploughing up grassland, cashing its stored fertility with a few years of arable crops, and then laying it down to grass again) was discovered in the eighteenth century, so maybe in some century to come the principle of *forest-ley farming* may be discovered. This will be the afforesting of land, harvesting of the ripe crop of trees perhaps a century later, some decades of arable and

26

grassland farming, then afforesting again. But this will not happen until mankind has learned to think ahead in centuries, not in periods of a year or two only.

The next step was the introduction of metals, first bronze and then iron, which enabled the thick turflands of the unforested country to be tackled. (Early man first occupied the unforested downlands in England—but he was a hunter and herder rather than a farmer.) Lynchets or lynches, which are terraces or benches which run more or less horizontally along the sides of the chalk downs, are the remains of the fields these late Bronze Age and Iron Age people made. They could practise a permanent and static agriculture—they did not clear and burn, plant and move off again, but kept the heart of their land by bare-fallowing (grazing animals on the resultant tumble-down grass), then ploughing up again and taking off more crops. No doubt they soon learned to carry out and spread the dung produced by such of their animals as were penned in the winter. They learned one thing that it took us until twenty or thirty years ago to rediscover—that is, that if you store undried grain in hermetically sealed conditions it will produce enough carbon dioxide to inhibit moulds and will not go bad. They harvested their grain by topping it with the sickle (either of stone or metal) and therefore could not store the grain 'in the straw' as farmers did later up until the invention of the combine harvester (*ricking* or *stacking* the straw

grain silo

27

with the grain still in it so that the grain dried out and matured naturally and did not *heat*, or go mouldy, as a heap of threshed grain will if not thoroughly dried). So they invented a method of storing grain (whether already threshed out and winnowed or still in the ear we have no way of knowing) in pits sunk in the chalk and covered with clay to keep the gas in. The rocket-like erections springing up in all the grain-growing parts of our countryside nowadays are a revival of this principle. They are airtight, and you can put damp grain straight into them and it will not heat or go mouldy. I have achieved the same aim by sealing grain in plastic bags. The rediscovery of this system has been made necessary by the combine harvester, which threshes the corn in the fields and therefore precludes the drying and maturing of it in the rick. My own belief is that this return to an Iron Age custom is retrogressive and that very soon we shall get back to rick-drying again—but here we leave the realms of history and enter into those of prophecy, and prophesying is a thing that every man should do for himself.

To get back to what we *know* has happened—not all combined grain is stored hermetically in this way. Grain grown in countries with a dry summer, such as Canada, comes from the combined harvester dry enough for ordinary storage in aerobic conditions, and much grain combined in Britain, where we have humid summers, goes through a grain dryer which (with enormous expenditure of power) dries it enough for it to be so stored.

But back to the Iron Age. Whether or not the Neolithic boys with their shifting *chena* cultivations in the lowland forests continued their migratory agriculture throughout the Celtic spread of stable farming on the uplands we do not know (my guess is that they did) but in about 100 B.C. a further great agricultural revolution occurred when Belgic tribes (also Celtic people) crossed the Channel to get away from the Romans, and brought with them, besides the potter's wheel and coinage, the wheeled plough. (The wheel itself, in chariots and farm carts, was probably introduced about two hundred years before this by people of the La Tène culture, or what we call 'Iron Age B'.) The heavy-wheeled plough enabled the Belgic people to invade the wooded lowlands, and this time permanently. They felled and burnt the jungle and, with their deep-ploughing implement, were able to keep the land in such subjection that the jungle never returned. Their ploughs were capable of mastering the heaviest clays, unlike the iron-shod but wheel-less ploughs of the 'Celtic A' (or Hallstatt Culture) Celts who arrived about 500 B.C., and the system of farming they introduced was a fertility-maintaining one and could continue on the same piece of land for generation after generation. It is notable that after the low country had been successfully conquered by the farmer (though why should we use such a militaristic term as *conquered* about husbandry which is the most pacific of all activities? The good farmer encourages and conserves other forms of life on his land and by using his brains and his inherited skills causes each bit of land to support more and higher forms of life than it did as wilderness) after the farmer *took over* the low country, it was then that the chalk downlands, and other dry, well-drained, naturally treeless areas, the only ones permanently farmed by the pre-Belgic peoples, went back to grass again and remained in grass right down to our own century. It was only in the First World War that some of the Downs were ploughed again, and then, alas, more of them in the Second World War and more even since then. Here again this return to Iron Age practice seems to me to be retrogressive. The centuries-old turf of the unploughed downland was very productive (for sheep and cattle grazing) but above all it was *stable*. It protected the steep slopes from erosion and was self-maintaining. The new ploughed slopes *look* wrong. They invite erosion (for the modern agribusinessman has not the wit of his Iron Age forebears to terrace the hillsides and thus guard against this) and indeed they are eroding very quickly. One generation though will make a lot of money out of them and, after that, well that's somebody else's worry, isn't it?

The Romans made little impact on British agriculture. The Belgic peoples whom they conquered were probably better farmers than they were anyway—didn't their swaggering Empire eventually collapse because with their *latifundia*, or huge estates, they ruined all their land?—and in any case the Romans didn't come in sufficient civilian numbers to create more than a scattering of isolated villas. They did drain some of the Fens though, and pushed the sea out of part of the Romney Marshes.

The English came next and they were a very determined and effective set of operators. It didn't take them long to drive the Celts into the mountains or kill them or enslave them and they introduced a variety of new crops, new forms of tillage, and a new, and much more highly organized, social fabric. They hacked their way into the toughest of the heavy-land oak forests and everywhere they went they set up their highly organized Open Field System, and it is easy to see (or it is easy to see after you have read *The Open Fields* by C.S. and C. S. Orwin) how this happened.

The English used heavy-wheeled ploughs pulled by long teams of oxen. The ownership of the oxen was cooperative: thus a team of six or eight oxen might be owned by three or four people or even more. Such a team (I prefer to call it a *span*, which is its name in South Africa where I first worked with oxen) could plough about an acre a day. Further, a long span of oxen is very cumbersome to turn round. Therefore the ploughmen would go on as long as they were allowed to, by the ground or their neighbours', before they turned round to come back. Thus each day's ploughing would tend to be an acre in extent but very long and narrow. A *strip* in fact.

Now imagine a span of oxen to be owned by Jack, Dick, Bill and Charley. What could be more natural than they should agree to go out and plough a strip for Charley first (he being the largest and worst-tempered, or maybe just the owner of more oxen than the others), then a strip next day for Dick, then one for Jack, then one for Bill who maybe only owned one ox. Then one for Charley again. And so on. And there would be other spans of oxen from the same village working, some of them owned perhaps by one rich man, and these too, every day, would go to the edge of the already-ploughed ground and plough another strip. As more land was won from the forest more strips would be ploughed, and by and large every man's holding would end up by being scattered in strips throughout the land of the village.

Now it may seem to us that this system would be intolerably in-efficient, as people had to dash about from one little bit of their land to another trying to farm it. But when we reflect that these people lived together in a probably fortified village anyway we can see that it was not as bad as we think. For nearly all the tasks that a farmer had to perform took about a day to do per acre, and therefore he would set forth from the village in the morning and go to one of his acre strips, work there all day and complete his task there, and return at evening and next morning walk out to another of his strips. He took no more time travelling therefore than if his land had all been in big blocks.

The strip system too had the advantage of fairness (each man had his share of good land and bad land) and also of flexibility. The young man, or the newcomer to a village, had the chance of saving up by working for a rich widow perhaps until he could afford to buy one ox, then work his way into a plough-team that was short of an ox, and thus acquire a strip or two of his own. Then in due course, by purchase perhaps, or by marrying the right girl, or by helping to clear yet more jungle, he would acquire other strips. If he had *one* strip he need never starve though, for in those early times of agriculture, an acre of land should have yielded him at least ten bushels of wheat, or about five times the seed he had put into it.

But, unless you are a modern agribusinessman with access to unlimited chemical fertilizers, herbicides and fungicides, you cannot go on growing wheat year after year successfully on the same ground. The wheat always takes the same elements out of the land, and further, you will get a build-up of the diseases and parasites that prey on wheat. Therefore the English soon learned to practise a rotation of crops and fallow (fallow is keeping the land bare for a period) and to do this, with their strip-system, they had to insist that all the strips in a contiguous area were cropped the same way. This was because they would, for example, let stock on to graze the stubble after the wheat had been harvested. Now if one man had had bare fallow on his strip while all the neighbouring strips had wheat, and wished to sow wheat himself in October, his crop would be trampled to death by all his neighbours' cattle. Fencing was expensive in labour and it was not possible to fence each individual strip.

And so the Three Field System grew up, enabling every strip to be treated the same in any one of the three great Open Fields. It was more convenient for everybody.

Briefly the system was:

Field A: Winter Corn (wheat or rye or a mixture of both). It was sown in October and lay dormant through the winter to grow early in the spring. It was the mainstay of the people's food. It was followed by a winter fallow.

Field B: Spring Corn. This followed the *winter fallow* after the Winter Corn. Thus, the latter was harvested in August and the empty stubble field (with the grass that had grown up among the stubble) was grazed by the collective cattle and sheep of the village until the land had to be ploughed in March and sown with the Spring Corn in April. The land has been thus partially rested, and manured from the dung of the grazing cattle. The Spring Corn consisted of oats, barley, beans, peas and vetches. The latter three crops, being legumes, greatly increased the nitrogen content of the soil, for legumes have nitrogen-fixing bacteria on their roots. The Anglo-Saxon cultivators doubtless knew this, but they had to grow some oats for their stock and some barley for that most vital operation—the brewing of ale.

Field C: Bare fallow. Nothing was grown on this field at all, after the Spring Corn of the previous year had been harvested from it. It was probably left to be grazed by stock during the winter, then ploughed as soon as it was dry enough in March, ploughed again in mid-summer, then ploughed a third time before it was sown to Winter Corn in October. And that is where we came in. The object of all the summer ploughing was to destroy weeds, for weeds could not be destroyed in the ensuing Winter Corn crop.

Now in addition to these three great fields, with their hundreds of personally held strips on them, there was the Common, which was a grazing ground for all the cattle, sheep and geese of the village, and which, if it was anything like the common grazing land you get today around North Indian villages, was lamentably overgrazed. Then there was the woodland, which provided *pannage* for pigs (that is they grazed in there and ate acorns, beech-mast, and whatever else they could find—and thus were fat after the autumn, when nuts were the most plentiful, and could be killed and salted for bacon). The woodland also provided wood for various purposes including firewood, and wild game.

The arrival of the Normans made little difference to this system of farming excepting in so far as even more was squeezed out of the farmers and consumed by the Lord of the Manor as the new *gauleiter* was called. The subsequent use of English words to denote livestock and Norman ones to denote meat—as ox beef, swine pork, sheep mutton—gives a clue as to who looked after the beasts and who ate them. As Lord Ernle remarked in his great book *English Farming*: 'Feudal barons are rarely represented as fumbling in the recesses of their armour for samples of corn.' The lords busied themselves with tilting and jousting, war for real, hunting, posturing about at court, intriguing and litigating, and the only thing they had to do with food was eat it.

The peasants meanwhile, were they villeins, serfs, freemen or bondmen, had plenty to do. The women, besides doing much of the field-work and nearly all the garden-work, keeping poultry and milking cows, had to card, spin, weave and make up wool into garments. They did the same for flax, also nettles which were an important source of fibre. They had to dip candles and make rush-lights, bake bread, salt meat, make butter and cheese. The men too did not give the Devil (who finds work for idle hands to do) much opportunity. Besides cutting wood for fences, putting up temporary fences to protect the growing crops, ploughing, harrowing, broadcasting seed, harrowing again, reaping, threshing, winnowing, taking the corn to the mill to be ground (it was the lord's mill of course and he got a great chunk of the flour that was ground), they had to kill animals, tan leather, make ploughs, rakes, harrows, spades and other implements, make harness and their own boots, carve kitchen and eating utensils out of wood, make fish traps and catch fish, and much of their time was spent anyway in doing forced labour on the lord's demesne.

In some ways though the medieval villagers might seem to us to have been fortunate. By and large they had plenty of land, for there were not many of them. And if their numbers increased there was always the forest, another chunk of which could be cleared, as long as it were not part of some royal deer-forest. The village was completely self-sufficient for everything it used. There must have been a strong and lively sense of community, for so many of the farming operations were done in common. In spite of the egregious exactions and taxations of the lord there appears to have been plenty of free time, for the holidays of the Church were many and most of these meant feasting if they didn't mean fasting, and often jollification. If somehow they could have done without the *lord* then they could, one feels, have had full and plenty, for only the limit of a man's industry was there to set a limit on the amount that he or his family had to shelter them, to wear, and to eat and drink.

After the Black Death in 1348–9 labour suddenly found itself in a seller's market. The Manorial System was already showing signs of change when this came about, for more and more peasants of various degrees were commuting their labour services to the landlord for money payments. In other words they started paying a money rent to the landlord for the use of the land which it may well be argued should have been theirs in the first place anyway, since it was their ancestors who had hacked it out of the forest, and their ancestors and themselves who had done all the hard work since to keep it that way. The barons and landowners too were needing more and more money, for more and more of them spent more time at Court, or at least in London, or travelling abroad. Also their wants in the matter of luxury goods, mostly imported from abroad, were becoming exorbitant. The Black Death, which carried off a third of the population, made it difficult for landlords to find tenants to work their lands, and this made it easy for new (and old) tenants to demand money payments instead of the hated labour services. It also forced the landlords to take land 'in hand' (i.e. farm it themselves—or at least through their agents) and the result of this, and the great demand that had grown up by that time on the Continent for British wool, was sheep.

From the mid-fourteenth century onwards the sheep-boom developed. When landowners saw they could make large fortunes with large flocks of sheep they became gripped with a fever that made them completely ruthless in enclosing the commons that should have belonged to all the villagers, enclosing the Open Fields themselves, and eventually, in many cases, simply driving out all the peasants from their estates, burning their houses, and turning all the ploughed land into sheep pasture. They could then run their estates with the small handful of shepherds necessary to look after thousands of sheep (there were plenty of gangs of unemployed roaming the roads, ever ready to help shear them).

Needless to say there were many peasant risings, but by one means and another they were all put down. The one that most nearly succeeded was led by Robert Kett, of Wymondham in Norfolk, a landowner himself and one who had made considerable illegal enclosures. Convinced by a deputation of displaced peasants that what he had done was wrong he told them: 'Whatsoever lands I have enclosed shall again be made common unto ye and all men, and my own hands shall first perform it.' He pulled his own fences down and thereafter led an uprising that came to control the whole of Norfolk and Suffolk, capturing Norwich by storm. He ruled wisely and benignly—killing not a single opponent except those few who were killed in fair fight—and it took an arm of nearly twenty thousand men, most of them German mercenaries, to defeat him. Kett was hanged alive in chains from the walls of Norwich Castle and captured peasants were slaughtered in the streets of Norwich until even Warwick, the leader of the King's army, was constrained to ask for a stop to the slaughter, saying: 'Is there no place for pardon? Shall we hold the plough ourselves, and harrow our own lands?' Heaven forfend.

So the enclosures, and the making of sheep-walks, as the vast tracks of depopulated country were called, went on; bread became dear, wages low, and gangs of 'sturdy beggars' roamed the countryside.

> Commons to close and kepe;
> Poor folk for bred to cry and wepe;
> Towns pulled downe to pastur shepe;
> This ys the new gyse!

as an anonymous ballad writer of the sixteenth century wrote, or:

> Sheepe have eate up our medows and our downes,
> Our corne, our wood, whole villages and townes;
> Yea, they have eate up many wealthy men,
> Besides widowes and orphane childeren;
> Besides our statutes and our Iron Lawes,
> Which they have swallowed down into their maws—

Till now I thought the proverbe did but jeste,
Which said a blacke sheepe was a biting beast.

(Bastard's *Chrestoleros*, 1598)

The manifesto of Kett's Rebellion was one of the most eloquent condemnations of all:

> The pride of great men is now intolerable, but our condition miserable.
>
> These abound in delights; and compassed with the fullness of all things, and consumed with vain pleasures, thirst only after gain, inflamed with the burning delights of their desires.
>
> But ourselves, almost killed with labour and watching, do nothing all our lives but sweat, mourn, hunger, and thirst. The present condition of possessing land seemeth miserable and slavish—holding it all at the pleasure of great men: not freely, but by prescription, and . . . at the will and pleasure of the lord. For as soon as a man offend any of these gorgeous gentlemen he is put out, deprived, and thrust from all his goods. . . . The lands which in the memory of our fathers were common, those are ditched and hedged and made several; the pastures are enclosed and we are shut out. . . . Whatsoever fowls of the air or fishes of the water, and increase of the earth—all these do they devour, consume, and swallow up; yea, nature doth not suffice to satisfy their lusts, but they seek out new devices, as it were, forms of pleasure to embalm and perfume themselves, to abound in pleasant smells, to pour sweet things upon sweet things. . . . While we in the mean time eat herbs and roots, and languish with continual labour, and yet are envied that we live, breathe, and enjoy common air! Shall they, as they have brought hedges about common pastures, enclose with their intolerable lusts also the commodities and pleasures of this life, which Nature, the parent of us all, would have common, and bringeth forth every day, for us, as well as for them?

But history was, in the end, behind the enclosers. The peasants, driven from the land, swarmed into the cities and obtained—some of

36

them at least—work in new industries. And, even in the sixteenth century, a new spirit was abroad: the spirit of agricultural improvement.

A great revolution was due to take place in farming. The unenclosed Open Fields and Commons of the manorial system were fine to provide food for a sparse rural population and on them a stable and self-sustaining agriculture had developed. But there was no room on them for individual experiment or enterprise. You *had* to farm your strips, on all three fields, the same way as everybody else. But, with the enclosures, the larger strip cultivators were enabled to compound their strips into one big enclosure each, on which a man could built a farmhouse and thus live on his land which is a prerequisite of good farming; thus they could farm as they liked. The smaller cultivators all went to the wall. They would find themselves landed with some tiny field miles away from anywhere, probably with no access, and would have to sell out at a pittance to a richer neighbour. But on the new enclosures enterprising men could farm well and try experiments. Tusser, who wrote *Five Hundred Good Pointes of Husbandrie* in 1573, was against the *champion* (Open Field Husbandry) and for the *severall*, which is what enclosed husbandry was called:

> More profit is quieter found,
>   (Where pastures in severall be);
> Of one seelie aker of ground
>   Then champion maketh of three.
>
> The t'one is commended for grain,
>   Yet bread made of beanes they doo eate;
> The t'other for one loafe have twaine
>   Of mastlin, of rie, or of wheate.

Mastlin was a mixture of rye and wheat. The point Tusser was making was that farmers on *champion* (the Open Field) had to put up with bean-bread for want of better, while a farmer in his own enclosure could enjoy twice as much good bread from the same acreage.

So the sixteenth and seventeenth centuries saw a great move from peasants living in villages to farmers living out, each on his own land, employing landless labourers for wages, and trying their hardest to produce good crops.

The big breakthrough was the invention of methods of feeding cattle and other stock during the winter. Hitherto the only winter food for animals had been a little inferior hay that could be saved from the wild grasses of the meadows from raiding stock in the summer, some oats, straw, barley and bean straw (wheat and rye straw is nearly inedible), and perhaps a modicum of oats or barley grain if such could be spared from human consumption. Therefore most stock was killed off every autumn and salted for winter. The result of this was that there was not enough dung from animals to fertilize the land.

Then trefoil or 'Burgundian grass' came in from the Netherlands, and rape for winter fodder or green manuring, and one William Turner, a herbalist, noted that 'the great round rape called a turnepe groweth in very great plenty in all Germany and more about London than any other place in England.' Barnaby Googe, in *Foure Bookes of Husbandry* of 1577, suggested that the 'turnepe' should come out of the garden into the fields. The carrying out of this suggestion, more than anything else, revolutionized English farming.

sheep folded on turnips

The turnip is a biennial; that is, it has the sensible idea of spending its first summer growing, storing up nourishment in its swollen root, lying dormant through the winter, then bursting forth early into flower and seed during its second summer so as to scatter its seed before its annual competitors get under way. Mankind learnt, in the sixteenth century, to make use of this characteristic, this stored energy, to keep and fatten cattle and sheep throughout the winter.

Gone was the annual massacre of beasts, sheep and pigs, and the necessity to live on salt meat until Lent put a stop to all meat eating anyway. With turnip cultivation it was possible not only to keep beasts, but to fatten them, all through the winter. Apart from improving the diet of the Englishman this brought about an enormous improvement to agriculture. For: 'A full bullock yard makes a full stack yard.' The enormous improvement of wheat and barley yields which was to follow in the 'High Farming' era of the late eighteenth and first half of the nineteenth centuries, and which was to raise wheat yields from half a ton an acre to as much as two tons, was due to the application of enormous amounts of farmyard manure. The system came about that a quarter of the arable land was put down to the new improved grasses and clovers to feed the animals during the summer and to make hay, while another quarter was put down to turnips to feed the animals during the winter. A third quarter was then devoted to the growing of Winter Corn (wheat, rye and field beans) and the other quarter to Spring Corn (barley, oats, beans and peas). The wheat straw all went into the yards to be trodden and dunged on by the fattening cattle, the oats and barley straw were fed to them, as were some of the oats and a little of the barley, but above all they were fed on turnips. This resulted in a vast tonnage of farmyard manure—the best 'compost' fertilizer that has ever been invented, that was taken out on to the land to increase its fertility. A benign circle set in—soil—plant—animal—soil—plant and so on. Coke of Norfolk, the great improver of the eighteenth century, would build any one of his tenants a cattle yard for no increase in rent—if the tenant would only agree to fill it, every winter, with cattle.

But these improvements spelled the end of the old slap-happy Open Field system. There was no place for turnips, or for careful grass and clover 'leys', on them. When all men's animals ran together on the fallows of the Open Fields or on the Commons there was no place for the man who wanted to improve his stock by better breeding, nor indeed to quarantine them from picking up diseases (a disease called *scab* was enzootic among sheep in the Open Fields).

39

The Open Fields system had to go. It is still preserved in one place in England though: Laxton, in Nottinghamshire. There for some extraordinary reason it survives, and is being preserved, and the holders of the strips are said to be very contented with it. They cultivate their strips with tractors, and apparently it works very well.

Across the Channel in France and the Low Countries the change was much slower, and various revolutions led to the peasants retaining their holdings, albeit they may have been consolidated. (In Holland the *rewelekawering*, or reallotment, of land so as to bring a farmer's land all together in one piece, is still going on.) The result is that the best peasant farming in France is as good as the best farming in the world, but it is a labour-intensive agriculture. The peasants of the Dordogne (as just one rather well-known example) produce as much food per acre as the most highly mechanized and chemicalized agribusinessmen of England or America, and they do it with a fraction of the *input* of oils, chemicals, and imported feed-stuffs. They do it, though, with a great deal of labour, but they are labouring for themselves.

England went the other way—to bigger and bigger farms, mostly farmed by tenants who rented them from huge estates, and employed very underpaid landless labourers. The labourers lived in 'tied cottages' belonging to the estate and, if they were sacked, were given a week to move out. Arthur Young, who was Secretary of Agriculture for the British government, a farmer himself, and a prolific and very sound writer on farming affairs, made three trips in France, both before and during the Revolution. He was a passionate advocate of big farms and an opponent of peasant farming, and yet many times during his French travels the admission was wrung from him that he had seen nothing better than peasant agriculture at its best.

The appearance of our countryside today is due to the Enclosures that started in the sixteenth century and were practically completed by the middle of the nineteenth. Enclosing landlords and tenants built stone walls around their new consolidated fields in the stony areas, and planted quickthorn hedges around them in the low country. Although the last thirty years have seen much bulldozing of both hedges and stone walls there are still plenty left, and the pattern of our land, seen from an aeroplane, is one of a cellular formation of hedged or walled fields with occasional woodlands.

The change that followed the High Farming period of the late eighteenth century and first half of the nineteenth (the repeal of the Corn Laws and consequent flooding of the country with cheap Canadian and Australian wheat brought the High Farming era to an end) was a change to tumble-back grassland (which means that fields were simply left unploughed so that they fell back first to thistles and weeds and then to inferior wild grasses), ruinous farm buildings, unhinged and rotting gates, unkempt hedges. By 1914 agriculture was in a terrible state. Then followed four years of high production during the war, with ploughing-up orders served on farmers to make them grow corn on what had been their grassland. After 1920 came the most disastrous depression with a complete neglect of home agriculture and a flooding of the country with cheap imports from all over the world (it is generally this period of utter depression that is taken as the 'before' of 'before and after' comparisons of crop yields by Ministry of Agriculture officials between 'then' and 'now'). Then the Second World War led, again, to a revival of agriculture. The horse was still king at the beginning of that war but American tractors came flooding in, and by 1948 horse-culture was not so much in retreat as in full rout—and the tractor spread everywhere. It was then that the next great change occurred. Ditches were piped and filled in, hedges were bulldozed out, trees and copses were swept

Ferguson tractor

41

away—all to make way for the tractor—which needed room more than anything else. The first tractors dragged their implements behind them like a horse dragging a cart. They needed great space to turn at headlands and therefore the fewer times they had to turn the better. Thank God Harry Ferguson came along and invented the three-point-linkage just in time. This was a method of mounting ploughs and other implements on hydraulic arms behind the tractor so that the tractor could back right up to a hedge and leave no headland at all. This saved many of the remaining hedges, because it became no longer economic to bulldoze them out.

calves in cubicles

Meanwhile post-Second World War agriculture had many other effects. It divorced the animals from the land. Instead of every arable farm having its big bullock yard, in which bullocks were fattened every winter on roots and straw, bullocks were reared and fattened in huge units on specialized farms, and their manure, instead of being the most important fertilizer, became an embarrassment and an expense to get rid of. Heavily subsidized (by government) artificial fertilizers, all imported, took the place of the High Farming muck cart. The old Four Course Rotation was dropped and monoculture—chiefly of wheat and barley—became the rule. Huge areas of land were turned over exclusively to these two white straw crops, and the place of the 'root break', or 'cleaning crop' (some crop drilled in rows that had to be hoed by hand and therefore acted as a weed-suppressing break) was taken by selective chemical weed killers—something that can be sprayed on a growing crop and that will kill weeds without too badly damaging the crop. The place of rotation of crops in keeping disease in check was taken by chemical sprays, which became stronger and more varied as the myriad strains of fungus, bacterial and virus disease organisms adapted themselves to survive under chemical attack. Successive strains of wheat and barley were bred by plant breeders to have resistance to the various diseases that monoculture inevitably brings but always they had to be superseded by more resistant strains as the disease organisms themselves adapted to attack the new varieties. So far the chemist and the plant breeder have managed to keep half a jump ahead of the diseases (many of

tractor with poison-spray boom

which we had never even heard of when I went to agricultural college!) but many farmers are beginning to be worried. But mono-culture is forced on the farmer by high wages, which force him on to machines, and by the enormous cost of machines, which force him to specialize. If he has to shell out ten thousand pounds for a combine harvester he can hardly afford to have a potato harvester as well. So he tends to grow all corn or all potatoes.

So we have the huge hedgeless areas of barley or wheat prairie

pig battery

where we used to have a hedged and wooded landscape. Take a copy of one of Constable's paintings and go and stand where the artist stood to paint it and you will see what I mean. Poultry have disappeared from view behind wire (and *on* wire) in huge windowless buildings. Pigs are fatted in total darkness except for the twenty-minute period three times a day when they are fed. Cattle are fatted in huge 'beef lots', spending all their lives on slats so their manure drops into huge 'slurry lagoons' below. Dairy cows exist in large herds (three hundred is common), fed largely on imported food from the tropics. Sheep still enjoy the free life on the hillsides (yes—suffering the extremes of climate that they were evolved to suffer and are very well equipped to take); and no man yet has found a way of fitting geese into a factory-farming system.

So admittedly a lot of the fun and beauty has been taken out of the countryside, and nearly all the fun of farm work, for a man either spends his life in the cab of a tractor (with ear-pads on to save him from going deaf) or putting milking machines on the udders of hundreds of cows even the names of which he never has time to learn.

There are still small mixed farms in existence, though. Some of the old yeoman farmers have managed to carry on, with what seems to them to be a healthy and less extractive agriculture, and you still see bullocks grazing in fields, or pigs rooting in an old orchard, and

threshing drum

even a pair of horses at work here and there. And the recent doubling of the price of oil, with its consequent doubling of the price of fertilizer, herbicides, pesticides and fungicides, has caused many farmers to pause and think. Highly mechanized and chemicalized agriculture is still economically possible. But what if the price of oil doubles *again*? Then maybe the hoe will have to come back to replace the herbicide, the muck cart the artificial fertilizer, and crop-rotation the pesticides. Let us hope the men and women will be found, when this happens, to wield the hoe and drive the muck cart. Otherwise there is going to be a great tightening of belts.

Chapter 3

The Bones of the Countryside

Like every country in the world Britain is changing shape in front of our eyes, although the term set to our vision is too short for us to notice it. Like an amoeba the dry land crawls and moves under the sky, sending protrusions out here into the sea, suffering loss elsewhere as the sea takes back, heaved up into mountains at one place and worn down by water and wind at another.

Wherever we go in our country we find that the scenery, the vegetation, the animal life, farming, culture, and customs of the people are what they are because of the rocks below. The very character of a man farming the Archean rocks of Anglesey is quite different from that of a Fenman who tills the flat deep silt-lands of Cambridgeshire. To understand the country we have to look beneath it at the rocks: all else is to some extent superficial.

In the Highlands of Scotland, in the Long Mynd in Shropshire, in Anglesey, in the Malvern Hills and in Pembrokeshire there are rocks that are so ancient that there are no fossils in them, for they were laid down before the dawn of life. So old is the world that there was time for the material that these rocks were made of to have bubbled up molten from the fiery depths of the earth; cooled into mountains; worn down by unimaginable eons of erosion, the powdered debris laid down at the bottom of lifeless seas; consolidated by the weight of miles of sediments laid on top of it to form some of the hardest sedimentary rock in the world; heaved up again as mountains by the convulsions of the planet—and the *last* of these things happened to them at least six hundred million years ago, and, in the case of some of the rocks in Scotland, perhaps as far back as *two thousand million years*, according at least to the informed guesses of geologists.

A few of these Pre-Cambrian sedimentary rocks, as they are called (notably the ones in Charnwood Forest in Leicestershire), have been found to contain traces of the very earliest forms of life yet manifested to us: very early and primitive forms of seaweed.

But to come down to earth, if we go to Anglesey and stand on the Pre-Cambrian rocks there, and then cross the Menai Strait and walk right across to the south-east of England, we will find ourselves crossing belt after belt of rocks; each belt becoming younger as we go south-eastward until we come to 'rock', which nobody but a geologist would call rock at all, laid down but yesterday.

We may be surprised at the comparative flatness and apparent

granites, lavas, etc.
Pre-Cambrian
Ordovician
Cambrian
Carboniferous
Permian
Silurian
Triassic
Jurassic
Devonian
Cretaceous
Eocene and Oligocene
recent

tameness of the landscape on those so ancient rocks in Anglesey, although the stone-hedged fields, desolate moorland and wind-scourged trees do give the island a feeling of great antiquity: a land made before the dawn of life. The flatness comes from a time when this part of the world had subsided and the sea cut into it, and planed down the mountains and made a large part of it one level. Anglesey is not infertile. The Welsh call it *Mon* and also *Mam Cymru*—the Mother of Wales—for it once supplied much of the Principality with wheat. Being fairly level and therefore without much water-power, it was a land of windmills—which have all been allowed to fall down, of course. There was one fine water-mill working until 1973, but the miller died and the mill has been allowed to go dere-lict—a sad disgrace.

Across the Menai Strait (which is a valley drowned by the sea when this country last subsided; the land is always going up or down in relation to the sea) we come to an area of planed-down rock similar to that of Anglesey but then—quite abruptly—the land soars up into high hills and we are in Snowdonia. Here much of the rock is Cambrian, from five to six hundred million years old and much of it is in the form of slate. Slate was once shale or mudstone, formed by fine silt or clay being deposited in the bed of a sea or lake and therefore nicely laminated horizontally. The shale was turned into slate though by being compressed laterally by great forces which have altered the laminations another way. The resulting metamor-phic rock then splits easily along the new laminations into the thin leaves which roof not only London and many big English cities but north and south American cities as well. Enormous quantities of this Cambrian metamorphic rock were shipped away in the last century to roof the cities of the Old and New Worlds.

Over the Cambrian in Snowdonia once lay a mighty sheet of vol-canic rock, which had welled up from the depths of the earth and spread out over the older sediments below. This happened in Ordo-vician times, from four hundred and forty to five hundred million years ago, and the molten rock solidified into a sheet of hard rock a mile deep. This in turn was worn away by the weather to expose the great area of Cambrian rock that makes the desolate barren Rhinog mountains. In a few cases, caps of the hard igneous rock have remained, as for example the peak of Snowdon and the peak of Cader Idris.

Having clambered up Snowdon then (or gone up it in the funicular railway!) to pay our respects to this Ordovician outburst, we continue on our way south-east until we come to the great belt of Ordovician rock, laid down when the whole of north and central Wales, except for the island of Snowdonia, was under a sea near a shore, into which vast quantities of mud and grit were washed by rivers; and it is this mud and grit which make up the shales of most of Montgomeryshire, Cardiganshire, Carmarthenshire and Pembrokeshire: most of Wales, in fact. Part of Snowdon itself is made up of a narrow belt of this Ordovician sediment (nothing is simple in geology) and part of it also of the Cambrian slate—and large slate quarries go far up the side of the mountain.

But a vast part of Wales is made up of regular waves of mountains of Ordovician shales, waves all about the same height (indeed if you stand on a 'wave' slightly higher than the others you can feel that you are looking over a mighty solidified ocean). These ridges are mostly rough sheep pasture, varied by growing spruce forests, and the valleys in between are fertile pasture and sometimes ploughland. It is in the valleys that the Welsh race has developed in its own peculiar way, retaining an age-old language and fostering a poetry and a music second to none in the world.

Continuing south-eastward we reach a belt of Silurian shaly rock, laid down four hundred million years ago in a warm sea which abounded with the newly developing invertebrate sea creatures. This Silurian episode sends a narrow tongue south-west as far as Llandeilo in Carmarthenshire. On south-eastward we enter the later Silurian Limestone on the Welsh-Shropshire border—a kindly farming land, if with a rather high rainfall.

Herefordshire is mostly made of the Old Red Sandstone of the Devonian period (from four hundred million to three hundred and fifty million years ago) which sends a long narrow tongue south-west all the way to the sea in Carmarthenshire and further west in Pembrokeshire. The 'Old Red' was laid down when a great desert continent (called by geologists the Old Red Sandstone Continent) had risen up across the middle of England and the detritus from this was blown, or else washed by the infrequent torrential rains of the desert, into what is now Herefordshire, much of Brecknockshire, and parts of Devon; lovely, gentle, undulating, well-drained and kindly country this is too. Men who farm the Old Red Sandstone have an unfair advantage over the rest of us. It was in this Devonian period, incidentally, that the first vertebrate fish appeared in the waters.

If we veer now southwards into the Forest of Dean, or northwards into the Black Country (that small but distinctive urban area that lies between Birmingham and Wolverhampton and nowhere else—it is quite wrong to lump the whole of the industrial north into the 'Black Country')—we come to a country of the next great geological age: the Carboniferous. This occupied the vast stretch of time between three hundred and fifty and two hundred and seventy million years ago. It was in this period that the Millstone Grits were laid down over large areas of what we now call the Pennines, in parts of north Devon; and the other Carboniferous limestones, or Mountain Limestones as they are sometimes called, which make the softer, less rugged country in the north of England. There is a great contrast between the sombre Millstone Grit country around Macclesfield and the softer, kinder country of the Mountain Limestone of the Dove Valley area, and the same contrast can be seen north of Skipton in Yorkshire. Both Millstone Grit and Mountain Limestone are stone-wall countries, but the Grit is sombre and grey and jagged while the limestone is white. The latter is a purer limestone, laid down in the bed of a deep clear sea. The Grit is a mixture of coarse sand and limestone and must have been deposited near the land from which grit and sand were being washed to mix with the marine organisms whose shells and skeletons formed the limestone. Kinder Scout is formed of the Millstone Grit, and austere and barren it is too.

After the limestones were laid down by the early Carboniferous seas came a period of the greatest importance to England and Wales today (not to mention Scotland) in which the land emerged from the sea, but only just, and was then subjected to a very gradual sinking process. This happened when the climate was damp and tropical. For thousands of years at a time the flat land would be just above water-level, great lush forests would grow in the swamplands, trees and other vegetation would die and fall and rot—but rot under anaerobic conditions to form an acid peat. Then would follow a period of rapid subsidence when the sea would come in and drown the forests and hundreds of feet of new mud would accumulate on the buried peat. Pressure would turn this into coal. Then the rate of subsidence would slow up, the sea-bed would emerge above the waves again, more forests would grow, more peat would be formed. Then there would be another long period of quicker subsidence with more deposition of mud. This went on in fairly rhythmical succession to form the thin layers of coal, pressed between large thicknesses of mudstone or shale, that we are mining today. In a book about 'the countryside' we scarcely need to consider the areas in which productive coal measures outcrop or lie near the surface, for these are almost without exception urban and not rural. The Forest of Dean is an exception to this, and so are the anthracite measures of south Pembrokeshire. In these areas the ground is so faulted and broken-up that only small-scale—often 'one-man'—mines could be supported.

But it must be remembered that the areas of any formation that we see on the surface of the ground, such as we have been considering, are not the whole story. The layers of rock slant up or down on top of each other (most of them are tilted by earth movements in the past) so that productive coal measures, for example, may lie thousands of feet under other formations hundreds of miles from where they *outcrop*, or come to the surface. Thus there are coal mines in Kent, a hundred miles from Warwickshire which is the nearest place where coal measures outcrop. The Kentish coal measures are deep down below other, and later, depositions. A huge coal seam has recently been discovered by deep drilling north of Selby in Yorkshire, underneath the much later Triassic rock, and even in rural Oxfordshire huge deposits of coal have been discovered far below the surface.

The first amphibians crawled out of the waters in Carboniferous times.

But to continue our south-eastern ambulation, from the Carboniferous we should, in theory, come to a belt of Permian rock, laid down from two hundred and seventy million years ago when we gather that Britain was a very hot desert near the Equator (yes, the continents move and we move with them, and the very earth twists to change its axis). But we would have to strike far north to find the

Permian, for it is missing south of Nottingham—which rather spoils the succession of our stroll. But a narrow belt of Magnesium Limestone runs north from Nottingham to Catterick, and on the coast of County Durham we get Magnesium Limestone outcropping again, and there—if we drill into the ground—we may get salt, gypsum, anhydrite and potash, laid down in the bed of the drying, dying, ultra-salty Zechstein Sea which once stretched over from Germany. The story of the life of this dying sea is sad and moving. The little animals which lived in it cut off from Mother Ocean, had to become more and more adapted to saline conditions as the water dried away and the sea became saltier, so that they became stunted and misshapen in their despairing effort to evolve new forms that could survive, until, beaten at last, they died out and the Zechstein Sea became as barren as the moon. The great potash deposits that are now being mined four thousand feet below the Cleveland National Park were laid down by this sea, as were the salt measures below Middlesbrough. The salt below the Cheshire Plain is found below the Triassic Red or Keuper Marl, laid down in another drying sea or lake. The saltiness of Cheshire cheese is said to be due to the natural saltiness of the Cheshire pastures over this Red Marl (I think it is due to the fact that the Cheshire cheese-makers add more salt to the curd). Certainly the flat Cheshire Plain, with its high rainfall, forms the most concentrated dairying area of Great Britain, where the cow is almost worshipped, and where the clothes a farmer wears, the make of car he drives, the company he keeps and the bar he drinks at at the pub are carefully and rigidly fixed for him by the number of cows that he owns! A twenty-cow man does not expect to be asked to supper by a hundred-cow man, although he may talk to him as man to man over the fence. It is strange to reflect that such complex social attitudes were decided on the bed of a dying lake two hundred million years ago.

But in our slanting walk across England we will miss the Permian and come straight into the next age: the Triassic, with the Late Triassic Keuper Marl which has the city of Worcester on its broad plain, and which slants right up England taking in most of Birmingham, most (as we have seen) of Cheshire, much of Staffordshire, the whole of the green low-lying Trent Valley, to narrow out and outcrop at the sea at Teesmouth. It forms a pleasant, undulating country, with some flat plains, and with many streams, rivers and canals in which at weekends the Industrial Briton tirelessly angles for fish which he considers inedible and puts back in the water.

We will by now have noticed that the belts of rock formations, which get progressively younger as we go south-eastwards (they can be dated roughly by radiological methods as well as by their fossils), slant up England from the south-west to the north-east. Obviously what has happened is that they have been laid down one on top of another, tilted violently by some grand upheaval, and then worn down towards the centre of the earth under the later layer to the south-east of it.

The next belt we come to—the Jurassic belt—is a prime example of this. Its outcrop slants right up across England, starting in the south-west at the coast near Lyme Regis and ending at the cliffs of Cleveland in north Yorkshire. It was laid down from one hundred and eighty to one hundred and thirty-five million years ago: a very important period for the development of animal life on this planet.

There are at least eleven readily identifiable zones, or layers, of Jurassic rock in England, starting with the oldest—the Lower Lias—and ending with the Purbeck Beds. They were laid down under the sea at a time when marine life was evolving so quickly, one species succeeding another, that it is possible—indeed very easy—to date the successive layers of Jurassic rocks by the enormous number of fossils in them. It is for this reason that the English Jurassic has been called the 'Nursery of Geology'. The Jurassic Age was the great Age of Reptiles, and most of the remains of giant reptiles have been found in Jurassic rocks, or the immediately succeeding Cretaceous. To be able to read the Jurassic successions like an open book in England one needs only to go to either of the two ends of the outcrop—where it reaches the sea in north Yorkshire or where it reaches the sea on the Devon-Dorset border.

But in our walk across England we will first become aware of the Jurassic by coming to a low-lying muddy area which forms the Vale of Severn. This very fertile land lies over the Lias: a well-stratified rock of alternate shales and marlstones. The Lias runs roughly from Lyme Regis through east Bristol, Gloucester, Rugby, east Leicester and Scunthorpe; and north of the Humber it dwindles to a thin line. It is generally low and muddy (easily washed away) and given to lush, fattening cattle pasture.

Having squelched our way over the low-lying Lias belt we come abruptly to a high, steep escarpment of a much harder rock, that overlies the Lias and has stood up to weathering much better: the Oolitic Limestone. Whatever the muddy sea conditions that gave rise to the soft Lias, they turned to clear seas at the bottom of which could form limestone—that is the remains of sea creatures that had manufactured limy shells or skeletons for themselves. In the Oolite one frequently comes on rock formed almost entirely of extinct shell-fish shells.

The western escarpment of the Cotswold Hills (which hills are nearly solid Oolitic limestone) is steep because the great sheet of hard limestone is tilted so that it dips gently south-eastward and its top (western) edge is left waving, as it were, in the air, only badly supported by the soft Lias rock beneath it. The Lias washes away, leaving the limestone unsupported, and the latter crumbles and crashes and the escarpment thus progressively retreats eastwards. This process is so slow that we are unlikely to see any stage of it happen in our lifetime.

Having sweated our way to the top of the escarpment we find ourselves on top of the Cotswold Hills. The valleys in these hills can be very beautiful, well-wooded with beech and ash and other lime-loving trees, and embellished with villages as beautiful as any villages in the world. Their beauty is due to the fact that they are built of the Oolite, which is a charming honey-coloured freestone, and built in the ages of good taste by fine craftsmen without the interference of any architects.

But on the top, out of the valleys, one stands not on anything the least like 'hills', but on a bare, not very fertile, almost flat (but gently sloping towards the east) landscape, with large stone-walled fields with a few windswept thorn trees growing here and there out of the stone walls, thin greyish soil—the whole great slab of limestone whipped, one feels, by winds which come straight from one of the cooler parts of Siberia. It is light shallow soil—in horse days three horses would pull a two-furrow plough. I have ploughed on the

Cotswolds with the plough-sole scraping along on top of the hard limestone beneath the soil. It grows fine malting barley (you don't want rich land to grow good malting barley), and traditionally the root break was turnips folded off to the heavy long-fleeced Cotswold sheep. The treading and dunging of the sheep 'did' the land, as farmers say: in other words, did it good.

This Oolitic limestone belt, which starts in the south between Bridport and Abbotsbury, slants nor'-nor'-east until it fizzles out just north of the Humber. Northamptonshire has a broad belt of it, often so laced with iron that it is reddish in colour and is quarried for iron ore, and the Oolite forms the spectacular straight edge of Lincoln Cliff. North of York there is another similar rock, but much thinner, and much mixed with shales, ironstones and grits. Something had clearly gone a bit murky with the otherwise clear Oolitic Sea up there.

Plodding our way down the bleak Cotswolds (don't get me wrong, Cotswold-lovers—I know the *valleys*, where the splendid little villages are, are not bleak, but I did spend the very cold winter of 1932 tending sheep on turnips near Aldsworth so I know what bleak means) we come to where the Oolite disappears beneath the later Jurassic rocks, with names like: Cornbrash (*brash* means shaley rock with bits of limestone in it—*corn* means good for growing corn), Oxford Clay, Corallian Rock (laid down in a coral-filled sea) and Kimmeridge Clay. The Kimmeridge Clay is the last of the Jurassic succession here and disappears beneath rocks of the next great age— the Cretaceous.

The Cretaceous, which formed so much of England (though none of Wales) lasted, according to somebody's wild guess, for some sixty-five million years and ended just seventy million years ago—to geologists just the day before yesterday. It saw the last of the great dinosaurs and the first of the warm-blooded birds and mammals, and the development of primitive fish into fish very like our cod and herrings. The Hastings Beds (a soft sandstone), the Wealden Clay which makes the Weald of Kent such a sticky place, the Greensands which ring the Weald and also form a narrow sickle-shaped belt from the English Channel near Sidmouth and Seaton right up to the Wash, under it, and then to Lincolnshire: these were all laid down under

Cretaceous seas. The Lower Greensand is well-drained, rather barren country, much given to pine trees, heathland, and stockbrokers' villas. The Upper Greensand can be very fertile, giving rise to a fine soil farmers call 'Foxmould'. Thus can conditions in a sea a hundred million years ago affect the incomes of farmers of today.

The Greensands disappear underneath the chalk, which forms, or at least underlies, a great part of England. The shallow seas near the land which must have given rise to the earlier Cretaceous rocks gave way to a deep clear blue sea with no detritus coming into it— maybe the land was far away or maybe it was desert so that little mud and sand washed from it. This geologists call the Great Chalk Sea, and it covered a large part of what is now Europe and deposited a great thickness of chalk at the estimated rate of about one foot every thirty thousand years. You have only to stand and look at Beachy Head, Flamborough Head, or Shakespeare Cliff at Dover to be amazed at the thickness of a deposit laid down with such incredible slowness—but there it is.

Even the Welsh hills (except Snowdonia) were probably covered with the chalk, but when they were heaved up again by some earth movement the chalk was washed away and denuded and not a scrap of it is left anywhere west of the great Jurassic Belt across England.

The chalk hills are thin-soiled, covered mostly with a springy turf delightful to walk upon, the valleys are for the most part waterless, for the chalk is absorbent, there are beech woods called *hangars* clinging to the lower slopes of the Downs, oak woods where pockets of clay-with-flints or other non-calcareous soil have been deposited on the chalk, and nowadays, sadly, much of the Downland, which should be sacrosanct from the plough, has been ploughed up to grow poor crops of barley flogged on with large doses of nitrogenous fertilizer. Sadly, because erosion is inevitable, and the Downs should be reserved for grazing sheep and cattle, for which they are excellent.

South-eastward-ho again and we hit the Eocene—pebble beds and sands and clays laid down on top of the old eroded chalk in the estuary of great rivers that were flowing slowly down from the plains that then covered the north of England and Wales a mere sixty million years ago. The London Clays which underlie most of the Wen (London) and Essex are of this period as are the Bagshot and Bracklesham Beds, which make up what Cobbett (who first named London the Wen) denigrated as the 'spewey gravels' of Surrey: gravels as he fulminated 'only fit for the villas of tax-eaters and stock-jobbers'.

The Oligocene Age is sparsely represented in England by deltaic deposits in the Hampshire Basin and the Isle of Wight, the Pliocene by some tiny pockets around Aldeburgh in Suffolk, and on the south slopes of the North Downs. But it was in the Pliocene that the great earth movements occurred which heaved up the present mountains of Wales and the North of England.

The Pleistocene, or *now*, has mostly been occupied by the Great Ice Age, and we are probably living in one of the brief interglacial periods. So far Pleistocene deposits are represented by the Sandling Country of Suffolk, sandy and muddy deposits of East Norfolk, and by the Crags, which are shelly sands laid down in what must have been the North Sea. Most of East Anglia though is covered by glacial drifts laid down by the great glaciers (and so is much of the rest of England), so we often have to dig down or drill to find the basic rock that lies beneath.

The Weald of Kent once underlay the chalk, was heaved up by earth movements, the chalk worn away to expose the softer Wealden material, and the North and South Downs are what is left of the chalk dome.

If we had turned and walked into the dead end of the West Country we would have found large areas of Devonian Rocks in Devon (it is a tribute to the primacy of British geologists that geologists all over the world have to use British names for their rock formations—there are no others). The great granite outpourings of Dartmoor, Bodmin Moor and Cornwall so heated and crushed the surrounding sedimentary rocks that they changed them beyond recognition into Schists and other metamorphic rocks. The granites themselves have decayed in Cornwall to form China Clay which is extensively mined. Veins of metalliferous rock have welled up from great depths into fissures in the granites of Land's End and other places and have been mined since time immemorial for copper and tin (the raw material of the Bronze Age). At the Lizard Peninsula is a strange outpouring of intrusive and metamorphic rocks, including the mysterious and beautiful Serpentine. South Wales has a large area of

Carboniferous: coal measures overlaid with the barren Upper Coal measure in which the coal starts as good steam coal in the east but gets harder and more metamorphosed as we go west until it becomes anthracite in the Swansea area and even harder anthracite in Pembrokeshire. Recent oil drillings in the Bristol Channel have revealed huge anthracite deposits off Pembrokeshire, four thousand feet deep under the sea south of St Govan's Head.

St. Govan's chapel

Pembrokeshire is protected from the sea by another great explosion of Igneous Rock, such as the Preseli Bluestone (not actually on the coast—but it was chunks of this, weighing forty tons, which were dragged to Stonehenge by very early man) and there are pre-Cambrian Rocks there of unimaginable age. The Lake District is an eroded dome of Ordovician and Silurian (i.e. very old) sedimentary rocks with massive granite intrusions from below. A large area of Early Carboniferous Rock (mostly Millstone Grits) and Coal measures covers the north of England.

The bones of the Lowlands of Scotland are very complex: a big area of Silurian mountains in the south, then a belt of Ordovician, and—north of a mighty fault—the Carboniferous which makes up the coal-fields of Scotland. There are patches of Permian there and big granite intrusions. North of another great fault which slants right across the country is the vast mass of highly metamorphosed (i.e. changed) pre-Cambrian rock, so fiercely contorted that often layers of it are upside-down having been pushed right over on themselves. These ancient and contorted bones make up a rugged and austerely beautiful countryside, the human inhabitants of which have been mostly driven out by the landowners, in favour of sheep, deer and grouse which are more profitable than human beings.

Chapter 4

The Buildings of the Countryside

As with other things, to see what the buildings of different periods of our past were like we have only to travel to more primitive parts of the world today. The countryman's house of the Neolithic Age, Bronze Age, Iron Age, Dark Age, Medieval Age, Tudor Age, and later, has its modern equivalent somewhere in Africa, the Far East, or elsewhere.

Neolithic and Iron Age Man probably lived in circular houses very like the round African huts of today. The latter vary from place to place, but most of them consist of a circular fence of sticks stuck into the ground, plastered with mud, or a mixture of cow-dung and mud, and roofed with a conical frame of sticks thatched with grass. The roof is generally built and thatched on the ground and then lifted onto the house. An African family, helped by friends, will construct such a house in a day. Which reminds one of the *tai-un-nos* or houses-of-a-night that were built by Welsh people of a generation ago on common land. If they could finish the house in a night and have smoke coming out of the chimney by morning they could keep the house, and the land on which it stood. Some loophole like this should be made in the present Town and Country Planning Laws which are stifling all natural development in the countryside!

As for materials, on areas where loose stone abounded, obviously stone walls would take the place of stick and mud ones, the stones being cemented together with mud. The house I live in in Pembrokeshire was built in exactly this way. In other areas where there were no easily found stones, walls were built up from the ground of mud, sometimes mixed with straw to bind it, and as long as the mud was not exposed to water it would last for centuries. Many of the *cob* buildings of Devon, Dorset and other counties, are built of just this. The footing of such a wall must be dry, it must be protected by an overhanging roof, and on the outside by white-washing. The picturesque overhanging thatch-roofed cottages in Devon villages with their white walls were not built that way just to look pretty for tourists.

Stone varies enormously and affects the nature of the buildings that are built with it. The great division is between freestone, and massive rock or non-freestone. The former is stone that was laid down in layers and stressed later so that it splits easily, not only along its natural horizontal beds, but also vertically at right angles to its horizontal splitting. It can thus be easily 'dressed' or cloven into rectangular blocks. Portland and Purbeck limestones are examples of this. Obviously it is much easier to build with freestone than it is with other varieties—for the latter come in all shapes and sizes and may be very difficult to cut. Walls of freestone may be thinner, they are straighter, and the builder has much greater control over his material. The great blocks of riven limestone that make up the buildings on the Isle of Portland are a supreme example (although the walls are not thin) and it is a disgrace of our reach-me-down age that modern houses are being built there now of brick, concrete ,and other pinchbeck materials. The Oolitic Belt (mostly the Cotswolds and Northamptonshire) provides smaller, less massive, and more variable freestone, and very delicate, well-designed, nicely finished buildings are the result. The stones are finely graded into different sizes, and even the roofs are built of the same stone split into tiles, graded so that the larger ones are near the eaves and progressively smaller ones up towards the top—this grading done for no other reason than appearance. There are other fine, easily worked building stones up and down the country: limestones, sandstones, grit stones, slates etc., and they always lead to civilized-looking country houses and farm buildings. We people who live in areas of igneous stone (stone that has welled up from the depths in a molten state) have to do with rock of all shapes and sizes, very often rounded by glacial action, and you try building a wall with footballs! The result is thick walls which are really a mixture of an infilling of mud, or mud-and-lime, and boulders, making rather primitive-looking houses.

In areas where there is no other stone, flint has been used on a large scale for buildings. Flints are accretions of siliceous material that have formed in the chalk (some say around sponges) and when the chalk is worn away they come in all shapes and up to the size of a man's chest. When they have been rolled about at the bottom of a river or in the sea they are round or kidney-shaped. In north Norfolk, parts of coastal Suffolk, and coastal Sussex, many country buildings are built of them and these have a lovely, tweedy, rough look about them and splendid tones of white or black or bluey-grey. It is hard to build with flint and almost impossible to make corners, so that the latter in flint buildings tend to be of freestone (brought from afar) or brick. Some of the mighty barns in north Norfolk (along the 'Flint Coast') are among the splendid buildings of the world. The Paston Barn is famous, but there are many others: the one at Trunch, for example. Most of the marvellous churches of East Anglia are built of flint—with quoins and other embellishments of Oolitic Limestone from Barnack in Northamptonshire (brought by water) or freestone from Caen in Normandy which probably came as ballast in ships. Flint can be *knapped*, or struck with a hammer to knock off a flat face, and *flushwork* of knapped flint, with the flat faces showing, often intermixed with freestone, was an art form.

In places with no freestone but plenty of oak woods 'stud and plaster' was the rule. The Cheshire Plain, large parts of the muddy

timbered house - Moot Hall Aldburgh

Midlands, much of East Anglia, gave rise to this. Timber framing (the 'studs') was built up to leave square panels to be filled in Cheshire and the Midlands and vertical oblong ones in East Anglia, and the spaces infilled with lath and plaster. The laths might be withies (willow wands) or, more often, split hazel, and the plaster was mud, or lime and mud, often mixed with the combings of horses to bind it. Often the whole building was plastered over, but modern lovers of timber buildings have knocked the plaster off to expose the beams—which seem so hard now after hundreds of years that they appear to be immortal. Since bricks came back (their use was forgotten after the Romans left until nearly Tudor times) the lath and plaster has often been replaced with brickwork. Timber-framed buildings spread into Wales from England—particularly in Montgomeryshire—but peter out when the high mountains are reached and straight oak was no longer available but stone was.

In the coastal areas of Essex and Kent there is much weatherboarding—tarred planks nailed to timber framing. This was because timber ships from the Baltic put into the little ports in this area and softwood planking was cheap.

As for roofing: cloven freestone was used in many places where it was available (for example the Cotswolds and the Isle of Purbeck); slate, which cleaves into thin, hard, durable slabs was used wherever it occurred and was (and is) the roofing material *par excellence*. But of course all stone roofs require a strong framework of sawn timber to nail them to. Thatch does not suffer from this disadvantage: it can be laid on unseasoned round timber, cut straight out of the forest and not necessarily even particularly straight. The timber will season *in situ*—and if it bends about a bit, the thatch will give and it doesn't matter.

Thatch could be of many materials. Heather thatch is not unknown in some Highland areas; although one doubts its value, bracken has been used, but straw—either wheat or rye—is the most common. What is known as 'wheat-reed' in Devon and many parts of the country is simply wheat straw that has had the grain threshed out of it *without* bending the straw. This can be done by feeding the sheaves of wheat into the drum of a threshing machine and then withdrawing them before the straw itself is damaged. *Straw thatch* is wheat or rye straw that *has* been broken in threshing. By piling such straw in a large heap, wetting it thoroughly, and pulling handfuls of straw out of the bottom of the heap, it is possible to extract fairly straight and parallel straws for thatching. Threshed straw rooves won't last much longer than ten years, however. Wheat-reed will last perhaps thirty. And Norfolk Reed, the common reed which grows in the Norfolk Broads and anywhere else where land is flooded not too deeply with water (including even fairly salty water) is the best thatch of all. A good reed roof, if ridged, will last seventy years or more. You cannot form a ridge of reed though, and generally a sedge of some sort is used for this.

renewing a thatched roof

There are two kinds of thatch—I call them flat thatch and deep thatch—and they are quite different. Flat thatch is used in Africa for most dwelling huts, in the west of Ireland, and for thatching stacks or ricks. Flat thatch is laid almost parallel with the slope of the roof—one layer, perhaps only two or three inches thick—simply overlapping the one below it so as to shed the water. It only lasts two or three years and the cabins in the west of Ireland have to be re-thatched this often. As it only takes a day to thatch a cabin this does not matter.

Deep thatch is quite different. The straw or reed is laid almost horizontally, with just a slight slope downhill as it comes outwards. Thus the roof has to be nearly as thick as the straw or reed is long.

Invariably with deep thatch the ears of the reed are laid inwards. This thatch is much longer-lasting but is fearfully expensive in labour to put on, and expensive also in material: it takes an enormous stack of it to thatch a house.

In good husbandry nothing is wasted, however. When thatch is finished, and pulled off to be replaced, it is thrown into the bullock yard or the pig-sties to be used as bedding, trodden into manure, and carted out to fertilize the land, perhaps seventy years after it, itself, grew out of the land.

Other roofing material is earthenware tiles—either small and flat or the kind of big curling pantiles you get in Suffolk and which originally came from Holland. Tiles are comely, long-lasting, trouble-free, but need plenty of good seasoned sawn timber to support them. You see them, as you would expect, in the stoneless areas of the country. Caernarvon slate, in Victorian 'times, spread far and wide, being light, cheap, and easily put on, and bid fair at one time to supplant all other materials.

In our century, though, corrugated iron, which inevitably rusts, looks horrible, and lets the water in, has come to replace much roofing of farm buildings if not of farmhouses. Somehow the true Briton jibs at *living* under a corrugated iron roof—whatever the South Africans, South Americans or Aussies may do. (In those countries they roof *cathedrals* with corrugated iron.) Corrugated asbestos is one better (whatever horrible diseases the workers who mine it may die of) in that it lasts longer and does not rust. It does gradually decay though. There are new lightweight flexible plastic roofing materials now which don't rust at least, but nobody knows how long they will stand up to direct sunlight and other factors.

Now the farmer's *house* differs very much in different parts of the country, and when built at different periods of time.

In the upland areas there were (and still are) many small family farms, and the houses did not have to be very big. This gave rise to the typical Welsh *long house*, which consisted of a small dwelling house with a cow-shed, calf pens, sometimes stables, and pig-sties, joined onto it and all under the one long narrow roof. I live in a house of exactly this type. The dwelling part of the building generally consisted of two living-rooms, a half-loft over one (called the *croglofft* in Welsh), and there might be a dairy, for making cheese and butter, between the dwelling and the cow-shed. You can milk your cows, walk through a door into the diary and strain your milk, then walk straight through another door into your house and sit down in front of the great *simnai fawr*, or open hearth, without going out into the rain—a very sensible idea.

As we go east towards the English border we come to much larger farmhouses—some of them enormous in fact, and with enormous kitchens. We may wonder at the size of the families the old farmers used to have—until we remember what Arthur Lane the Drum said, in the first chapter of this book, about *men in the house*. These arable, or arable and grassland, farms had their unmarried workers living in the house and eating in the great kitchen, and that is why the houses are so huge. The great open fireplaces—burning logs that some-times had to be dragged in by horses—gave way in Victorian times to the open-fronted iron coal-burning ranges; in our time these gave way to the Aga or the Esse (insulated, enclosed coke- or anthracite-burning stoves) or to electric or gas ranges, with the gas coming out of bottles. The Aga is the cooking device of most larger farmhouses though, and the Rayburn in smaller ones.

66

Now there are no 'men in the house'. They went as Victorian 'respectability' came in, when the farmer and his lady wanted to ape 'the gentry'. Cobbett already saw this coming and he hated to hear 'the tinkling piano' coming from yeomen's houses.

> Man to the Plough
> Wife to the Cow
> Boy to the Barn
> Girl to the Yarn
> > And your rent will be netted.
>
> Man tallyho!
> Girl Pi-an-o
> Wife silk and satin
> Boy Greek and Latin
> > And you'll all be gazetted!

was an eighteenth-century jingle. Gazetted means gazetted as bankrupt. But anyway there came a time when there was no more room for common *workers* in the houses of gentlemen farmers. As we have seen in the first chapter, the custom of men in the house lingered longer in the west and north of England than it did in the south-east. In the north and west they were (and still are) more democratic. In Yorkshire or Lancashire or the Border country it is very difficult to tell master from man. In Sussex it is very easy.

Farm buildings vary too from period to period and from area to area, but there are good reasons for the variations.

Grain storage. We have seen the grain pits of the Neolithic cultivators, made necessary by the fact that they cut the heads of their corn off short with stone sickles and therefore could not store it in the rick, had no means of drying it, and so had to store it anaerobically so that its own gases would preserve it from moulds and decay.

With the iron and steel sickle, and later the scythe, there was enough straw on the grain-heads to make it easy to *rick*, or stack, the corn, either in the open under thatch, or inside a big barn. Storing in the barn saved grain from damage during a rainy harvest—because it could be carried straight in every fine day, whereas if ricked outside it would be exposed to the weather until the last load was laid on the rick and it could be thatched. Having been stored it then—(probably some time in the winter when there wasn't so much work to do) had to be threshed. This could be done in the open on a big sheet of canvas, but then only in fine weather. So arose the big corn barns—of tarred weatherboarding on timber framing in non-stone countries, flint in flint lands and stone in others—which were built with two transepts like Norman churches. They were built, in fact, in the form of a cross, and each transept had a huge door big enough to let a loaded wagon in. The doors were big enough, too, to let the wind in. The middle of the barn, between the transept doors, was the threshing floor, and there, all winter, the 'daymen', as the workers who were not horsemen were called because they were employed only by the day, hammered the grain out with flails. When they had hammered a lot they would open the two enormous doors and let the wind blow through, and would throw the grain and chaff up into the aid with big wooden shovels and winnow it. The chaff would blow out of the leeward door while the heavy grain fell to the floor. Chaff went, mixed with oats, to feed the horses; straw, if oats or barley, to feed horses and cattle—if wheat or rye, as bedding and later manure. Everything fitted into the ecology of the farm and nothing was wasted. The bullock yards would be close to the barn so that the straw could go straight there.

Tithe barns were to store the ten per cent of the crops, taken straight from the harvest field, that were the Church's due.

We've cheated the Parson we'll cheat him again!
Why should the old Parson have one in ten!
One in ten!
One in ten!
Why should the old Parson have one in ten!

was sung at harvest suppers, presumably ones to which the parson was not invited.

When the winnowing machine, and later the threshing machine, were invented, a new development occurred. Existing barns were furnished with 'horse gins' or 'horse gear' which transmitted the power of a horse or horses walking round in a circle. Some barns had (and still have) strange-looking circular structures with conical roofs built on to the side of them. These were to house the horse gins. A shaft went from them into the main body of the barn to drive the machines.

For centuries grain was taken to the windmill or water-mill to be ground. But in the late eighteenth and early nineteenth centuries more and more farmers fitted mills of their own—first stone and then steel plate mills—driven by water or horse gin, and in time by gas engine or heavy oil engine. Then the hammer mill came in and a new building was needed: the mill-house with granary over. If you see stone steps leading to the high door at the end of a building out of doors on a farm you can generally assume that the steps lead to the granary, which had a strong wooden floor with a chute in it to send the grain down to the mill below. In hilly countries with many streams you may often trace the remains of a water-wheel leat out the back of the building, and maybe even find the bearings of the water-wheel which has almost certainly gone to be broken up for scrap. Carrying sacks of wheat (2¼ cwt) up the granary steps was no job for a weakling and carrying sacks of beans (2½ cwt) was a back-breaker. But generations of farm workers did it without a murmur and in fact took a pride in being able to do it.

With the coming of the combine harvester (in Britain substantially after the Second World War) all this was changed. Instead of the grain drying naturally in the field, being bound into sheaves, stooked, then put into the rick to mature for months until it was needed, it was threshed as it was cut, and taken to the store in a damp condition. We were back in the Neolithic Age again with the problem of what to do with wet grain. At first the Neolithic solution was not thought of—that of storing damp grain in airtight pits—and so artificial drying was developed. If you see a windowless modern building on a grain farm with large circular ventilator holes in the walls it is probably a grain dryer. If it is a very big grain farm there may be a row of circular silos, maybe metal, maybe concrete, alongside it. All wheat for human consumption, all barley for malting purposes, and much grain for animals is still dried and stored by this method in this country.

The Neolithic solution was not rediscovered until a few years ago. It led immediately to those (some think rather elegant) silo towers rising out of the countryside. The larger stock farmers who grow their own barley simply pump it, damp as it comes from the combine, straight into these towers, seal them up, and the grain generates enough carbon dioxide to inhibit the moulds that would normally destroy it. The stuff is pulled from the bottom as required and rolled or ground (it doesn't grind very well) for pigs or cattle.

Grass and green fodder storage. Hay was normally stacked loose in the field or the farmyard (hagard) in neat well-shaped stacks and thatched with pulled straw or other material. The drawback to this is that when you take part of the thatch off in the winter to feed the hay, and pull some hay out, you have a job to stop the rain getting in to the stack and spoiling the rest. Hay barns were therefore sometimes built to take the loose hay so that it need not be thatched and you could help yourself without spoiling any. Small upland farms often had, and have, hay barns of stone roofed with stone or slates near to or attached to the cow-shed—often part of the Long House in Wales and Scotland in fact. When cheaper materials such as corrugated iron came in in the last century the so-called 'Dutch Barn' became widespread: a corrugated iron roof, sometimes pitched, sometimes half rounded, supported on wooden or steel supports, sometimes clad on one or more sides to keep the prevailing rainy wind from driving in. Nowadays, owing to government grants on such buildings, more finished and durable hay barns, often of asbestos cladding on steel frames or frames of reinforced concrete, are taking over. These have the advantage that they can be put to other uses, such as housing stock when not full of hay, and also that they give better protection than the open-sided hay barn for hay in bales. Loose hay will shed a great deal of water: baled hay quickly absorbs it and goes rotten.

'Dutch barn'

The *real* Dutch Barn, that you get in Holland (where you seldom see what British farmers like to think of as 'the Dutch Barn'), is a very sensible device. It has a circle or a square of tall poles which have a conical roof, often thatched, slung between them with ropes over pulleys. At haymaking the roof is hauled up, the hay piled on the ground, and after each day's work the roof is lowered so as to sit on the hay. Thus there is never a space between the top of the stack and the roof to let the rain in. When using the hay in the winter the same principle is applied. In Friesland, though, you get the enormous Fries farmhouse, which has a huge roof coming right down to the ground on each side so there are virtually no side walls, the cows, pigs, chickens and all the stock on the ground inside, the hay pumped by elevator into the huge loft over the animals, and the south end of the building taken over by the farmer's house. Thus the hay is handy for slinging down to the animals below; during the winter it acts as insulation to keep the animals warm. No doubt some of this warmth gets through the party wall into the dwelling house, in which the farmer has nothing but south-facing windows. I doubt if a better form of farmhouse has ever been devised: there is no scruff of farm buildings scattered about outside and only one roof to maintain. We could not even experiment with such buildings in this country because the planning laws would not allow us.

Silage has partly taken over from hay in the last half-century. This is the principle of consolidating freshly cut (or slightly wilted) green material, such as grass and clover, green maize or other fodder crops, so as to exclude the air, whereupon it ferments rather than rots and forms a palatable foodstuff for cattle which has much of the protein and other nutriments of the original material. It has the advantage that you can cut the material on a wet day, or at least in a brief interval of dry weather, whereas hay has to be dried in the wind and sun. In North America the silage tower is a common feature of the farmscape: a metal or concrete tower (looking much like the 'Neolithic' damp grain towers of Britain) into which the greenstuff is elevated and consolidated. In Britain the silage tower was tried back around 1900 by progressive large farmers, but has been more or less completely abandoned for the silage clamp with a self-feed face, although there are a few silage towers left. Basically the clamp consists of two low parallel walls of reinforced concrete or old railway sleepers, between which the greenstuff is stacked ('clamped') while a tractor is driven over it from time to time to consolidate it. When it is full, black polythene sheeting is put over it to exclude air and rain and weighted down with old motor tyres. Often the cows are allowed to help themselves to it through a row of movable pillars known as 'tombstones' which allow them to get their heads at the stuff but not trample on it. Also there may be a big asbestos building at one end of the clamp and covering it to shelter the animals. Beef animals are fattened in such sheds, on silage *ad lib* and barley, and dairy cows are sometimes kept through the winter at the silage face.

Cow Housing. Dairy cows were often milked out of doors by a fair maid with a wooden stool, two wooden buckets and a yoke to carry them on. They still are in parts of Holland and Scandinavia, and in Friesland you see boats being punted along the canals with small portable engines which drive milking machines on them. The cows are on islands and therefore it is impossible to bring them back to a cow-shed.

But the Welsh Long House, and in fact all upland farms, long ago had cow-sheds into which the cows were driven just to be milked twice a day and tied up and fed during the milking. Invariably there are small calf-pens in or next to the milking house. Sanitary rules in this century, combined with better concrete, brought about the improvement of a concrete standing for the cows, a gutter (or 'dunging passage'), behind them, a concrete feeding trough in front, partitions between every two cows, either chain or rope ties or galvanized iron locking devices, and sometimes small automatic water troughs. Nowadays there is generally an overhead pipe system which brings vacuum from a small electrically driven pump in a room at the end to operate the milking machines.

As cow herds got larger (a man must milk a hundred cows now to give him the standard of living that ten would have given him in 1945) the idea of being able to tie the whole herd up together in one building became impractical. Various kinds of 'milking bales' or 'milking parlours' were invented. The idea was that the cows would be collected in a big yard or shed, and put through the 'parlour' in batches of, say, four at a time, milked, fed a carefully measured quantity of 'concentrate' (high protein food), let out and another four cows let in. One man working in the parlour could milk up to a hundred cows in a few hours. Extensions of this idea have come, mostly from America, such as the 'cotel' (*cow hotel*—you can rely on the Americans for 'picturesque speech and patter'). This is an enormous revolving device, wherein the cows are revolved round two or more white-overalled technicians who spend their entire working lives clapping milking machines on cows' udders. They never see the faces of the cows.

Housing for other stock. It is difficult to identify the purpose of most modern stock buildings without going inside, for they tend to be multi-purpose buildings. Cattle are fattened under the big roofs with silage clamps at one end of them as I described. If the silage is clamped under the shelter of the roof often bales of hay and straw are stored on top of the silage. As the cattle eat their way into the clamp, the hay is thrown into hay racks for them and the straw flung on the ground. Often there is insufficient straw nowadays (because the farmers burn it) and the cattle are belly-deep in muck and spoiled silage. The 'beef lot' has come over from America—generally just a series of pitched iron roofs held up on poles. The cattle are kept in strawed pens under the roofs and there are passages wide enough between the pens for a tractor to get along pulling a trailer to bring fodder. Most cattle houses are empty in the summer, when the cattle are let out to grass.

A refinement in dairy cow housing in recent years, and quite a sensible one, is the *cubicle* house. On heavy wet land, and in the north and uplands, it has long been the practice to keep cows indoors all winter, for if you let them out they would only 'poach' (i.e. destroy with their treading) the grassland and would lose condition from the wet and cold. Nowadays, with very big herds, cows have to be housed all winter on all land, because if you drive a hundred-cow herd to and fro between the fields and a milking shed twice a day during the winter they will churn the fields up into a quagmire. The old custom (practised even in the primitive Welsh long house) was to keep the cows tied up each in her stall with straw or bracken bedding. Every so often somebody would have to fork out the spoiled straw and muck and put in clean straw. Now that straw is scarce (because burnt—but we will discuss this later) and labour is scarce, other methods of 'bedding' cattle have been tried. One is to keep them on *slats*. These are wooden slats with gaps between down which the dung falls, or is washed, into a slurry lagoon whence it is pumped into tankers which take it out on to the land again. It is a revolting job and there are severe objections to it: one of which is that when you turn the cattle out in the spring they do not like to eat the grass that the slurry has been sprayed on. The other method, which was only discovered some ten years ago, is to keep the cows loose in a large building with a concrete floor but allow them access to *cubicles*. The cubicles are simply cow-sized areas fenced off on three sides, and with insulated concrete pads for floors. The cows soon find that the insulated patches are warm, and that when they get within the cubicle they are safe from annoyance by other cows, and so when they want to lie down they automatically go into the cubicles. When they want to dung or stale they cannot do it in the cubicles (for they cannot *back* into them) so they do it in the dunging passages outside, where a tractor-driven scraper can take it away. There can be a silage face at one end of the shed, or any other feeding arrangements; no straw is required, the cows are warm and safe and although it looks as if they are lying on cold concrete in fact they are not, for the floor under them is insulated. This method, like the slurry lagoon, has the disadvantage though that the dung is not used for *activating compost* (i.e. turning straw bedding into manure) but has to be put straight on the land as raw shit, in which form it does not do so much good, and further makes the grass unpalatable. On the old mixed farm muck was put on the arable land during the root break and by the time that land was put down to grass again any unpalatability had long disappeared. But that system required *labour* which is the one commodity on the land in short supply. The modern farmer is forced to sacrifice nearly anything in order to achieve one thing: saving of labour.

We now come to the *Belsen house*, which in one form or another carries saving of labour to its highest form. We all know—or know of —the battery hen-house. In this, thousands or tens of thousands of hens are kept in wire cages. Their shit falls through the wire onto a moving belt which takes it away, another moving belt carries away their eggs, which roll by gravity out of the cages, another one carries food past their noses. They only last eleven months and are scrapped during their first moult because by then they have tumours of the liver and various other disabilities. You can buy them for a few pence apiece from the Belsen houses and when you do it takes them some hours to learn how to walk, several days to learn how to *scrap* (that essential art of the *genus* hen) and they are amazed when they find they can flap their wings and generally fall over the first time they do it. By law the wire pens have to be big enough so that each bird has room enough to stretch one wing—the framers of the law probably not being aware that a hen cannot flap one wing without the other.

Poultry for meat are generally kept nowadays in *deep-litter* houses. It was discovered, some time just before the Second World War, that if you keep birds crowded together on a considerable depth of litter—say straw—their droppings will cause the litter to ferment, produce heat which will warm the chickens and kill off harmful organisms, absorb very quickly the droppings of the birds, and generally act as an hygienic floor. The fattening birds are crowded into these sheds in subdued artificial light—if it is bright they kill each other because of the stress of overcrowding—and fed from hoppers. From the outside the battery laying-house cannot be distinguished from the deep-litter Belsen house. Generally both have a large metal hopper or two at one end. These contain the mash which is taken by conveyor belt to the birds.

The pig Belsen houses are like the poultry ones, only generally bigger and built of concrete or breeze-blocks. They are seldom things of beauty from the outside. Breeding sows are kept in small groups inside with a sleeping area and a dunging area—the former with an insulated concrete floor. When they are due to farrow they are confined, individually, in narrow crates in which it is impossible for them to turn round but in which they can just stand up and just lie down. When the piglets are born these are lured to one side, under the rail, by infra-red light, but they have access to the imprisoned sows' teats under the rail.

Pig-fattening Belsens look, inside at least, exactly like an old-fashioned prison. That is, there is a long corridor down the middle and cells on either side of it with light-proof doors, each door with an inspection hatch in it and an electric light switch by it. The fattening pigs are kept in their litter groups (i.e. ten or twelve in a pen) in total darkness except when the light is switched on for twenty minutes twice or three times a day for them to feed. The idea of the darkness is so that they do not move about and lose weight and do not fight owing to the intolerable boredom. The temperature is kept very high by good insulation and limited ventilation. Not all pigs are fattened in total darkness but an increasing number are.

Calf Belsens are houses full of cubicles in which a calf can just stand or lie but not turn round. If small calves are weaned too early from their mothers and kept in groups they will suck each other's navels for comfort and cause diseases, so they are kept in these individual cubicles. They are fed milk-substitute from a bucket or with various automatic devices.

I describe these various forms of Belsen house, although the process is distasteful to me, for they are a large and growing factor in our countryside. They may not be very obvious unless you are looking for them, for they are low, long, inconspicuous buildings with no windows. They might be army huts, or huts for prisoners of war.

Meanwhile there are plenty of old-fashioned farmers—and a growing group of a new kind of husbandman looking forward to new ideas—who still try to keep animals in conditions much nearer to the conditions for which they were designed by nature. You can often see sows—even on large farms—kept out on grassland or in woodland in movable arks, each sow allowed to farrow in her own ark on plenty of straw—and if a sow now and then lies on a piglet and kills it, what does it matter? You still see store pigs (i.e. young pigs growing before they are fattened) running out on fresh ground behind an electric fence, and then kept in a light airy shed, with plenty of straw to lie in and plenty of room to play, to be fattened. You still see hens kept in movable arks on grassland, where they can run about and do the grass and themselves good, even though they have to be kept shut in their houses until midday so that by then they have laid their eggs and these are not lost. But economic drives to have bigger and bigger farms, plus scarce and dear labour, have forced practices on farmers which they, in their hearts, know are wrong and which their forefathers would not have tolerated.

The graceful conical brick buildings called *oast houses* in the Kent, Sussex and Herefordshire countryside were of course for drying hops. They are now either falling down or have been bought by arty Londoners to be turned into quaint dwellings. The principle of all such drying kilns was very simple: a grid of either perforated tiles

oast
houses

or perforated iron plate, with a fire under it and the substance to be dried on top. Malting kilns, generally—in England at least—large-scale buildings but in Wales and Scotland often on a farm or small-mill scale, were the same. In the eighteenth century brewing began to be big business and thus there are many old malting houses of large size about the country, some from the late eighteenth century but most from the nineteenth. Ale, which is not made commercially in Britain nowadays, is made from malted barley not flavoured with hops. Beer is made from malted barley flavoured with hops. Hops came from Germany in the sixteenth century:

> Hops, Reformation, bays and beer
> Came into England all in one year.

Edward VI passed laws about hopped ale, or beer, and even in Henry VIII's time hops were frowned on but nothing could stop them and beer became the Englishman's favourite drink.

Briefly, beer is made by causing barley to germinate by wetting it and keeping it warm. This causes the starch in the grain (which is insoluble) to turn into sugar (maltose) which is soluble. When grain germinates this stored energy must be made into a soluble form before it can travel about the new plant. The maltose is steeped out in warm water and the resulting liquor has yeast (which is a microscopic plant) added and this consumes the sugar and excretes alcohol. So a maltings consists of a building of one or more floors on which the barley can be laid out, wetted, and allowed to germinate, and a kiln. The kiln is almost exactly like an oast house (hop-drying building) and therefore looks like one. Generally there was a cowl on top, which swung with the wind so that its aperture always pointed to leeward and caused a good draught. As a great deal of floor space was needed for the germinating process, the commercial maltings were multi-floored, the stories had very low ceilings (height was not needed because the barley was laid out in a shallow layer), shutters on the windows to retain heat and slate floors to resist the water and make shovelling easier. In all the grain-growing areas you will find old malting houses—some enormous. At Mistley and Manningtree in Essex there are huge ones, and Snape Maltings, near Aldeburgh, part of it now taken over by the Aldeburgh Festival Committee for a concert hall, is a superb example. Alas, malting is now conducted in chemical factories, which look like chemical factories (and the resultant beer tastes as though it comes out of chemical factories). The only proper working country malting I know is at Budle Bay in Northumberland. Malting went the way of milling—it got concentrated in the huge deep-water ports so that it could become dependent on imported corn.

Corn-milling is mostly done in the enormous port mills, but there are still a few small grist mills spread about the countryside. Many of these are in old watermills, the water-wheel now generally superseded—or at least reinforced—by electric or diesel power. Grist means corn ground for animal feeding stuffs. Water-mills were generally multi-storied buildings so that grain could be hoisted (by water-power—everything in the mill was driven from the wheel) to the top floor and allowed to descend by gravity to the milling floor, go through the stones, then descend to either the first floor to be bagged and lowered onto the wagons outside, or to the ground floor to be bagged. If it was bagged on the ground floor the bags had to be hoisted to the first floor to be loaded, again done by water power.

Water-wheels are not buildings but nevertheless we will consider them in this chapter. They are basically of three sorts: undershot, breast wheel, and overshot. The *undershot wheel* is applicable in streams which have a large volume of slowly moving water. The water is made to flow into a channel which has a rectangular section and the rectangle is almost exactly filled by the rectangular paddles of the wheel. The water has to push the paddles out of the way to get out and thus turns the wheel. *Breast wheels* are used when there is a fair *head* (difference in level between the water before it goes through the wheel and after). The water is discharged on to the wheel as high up as possible so that it fills buckets, turning the wheel backwards in the direction from which the water comes. An *overshot wheel* is one in which the buckets are built to face the other way and the water is shot over the wheel to turn it in the way it is going. In the nineteenth century many mills were fitted with turbines (there is a fine one, open to the public, at Blackpool, near Canaston Bridge, on the A. 40 going to Haverfordwest in Pembrokeshire).

Water-wheels and turbines also drove textile and other machinery all over the country. In the Frome Valley near Stroud in Gloucestershire the little river drove textile mill after textile mill—one every hundred yards or so—for several miles. One of these mills at least had five water-wheels and most had more than one. Fortunately the mill buildings in the Frome Valley have mostly survived, having been taken over by other industries, although water power in them has been superseded. The wool industry left East Anglia and the West of England for Yorkshire not because there was coal in the latter place —but because there was ample falling water. The industry had substantially moved north before coal power came into general use. There are still a few small water-driven wool mills working in Wales.

Another source of water power was the tide. There were tide mills at fairly frequent intervals around the coasts of East Anglia and the south coast. The one at Woodbridge in Suffolk is now being restored. The principle was to allow the tide to flow into a lagoon on the flood, then impound the water and let it drive an undershot wheel as it flowed out. It would go on turning the mill until the rising tide had again equalized the level inside and out, when the wheel would be stopped and a sluice opened to allow the flood tide to fill the lagoon again.

Water power had many applications. Pumping water from mines was an early one, as was driving mine-hoisting machinery, crushing machinery, etc. The many ponds created by earth dams in Sussex (called 'hammer-mill ponds') were to impound water to drive wheels which worked the blooming hammers of iron mills. The famous 'Lady Isabella' Wheel at Laxey, Isle of Man, is a fine example of a mining wheel. It was built in 1854 to pump water from lead mines. It had a circumference of two hundred and twenty-seven feet and was six feet wide and could pump two hundred and fifty gallons a minute from one thousand two hundred feet. It was a breast wheel.

Windmills were traditional in south-east England (there were hardly any in Wales except in Anglesey, and few in Scotland. Where you have falling water you don't need windmills) and of three types. The oldest existing kind is the *Post Mill*, which is a wooden structure mounted on a great central post. The whole structure pivots round on the post to face the wind so that the room with the stones in it, grain store, flour store—everything turns with every shift in wind. *Tower Mills* and *Smock Mills* work on quite a different principle. With these the tower of the mill is stationary, built of brick in the

Post
Mill

Smock Mill

Tower Mill

case of Tower Mills and weatherboarding in the case of Smock Mills
(the smock-like appearance of the latter gave them their name), and
only the cap, carrying the sails in front and the fantail (a fan at right
angles to the sails which, when side-on to the wind, activates
machinery for turning the mill sails-to-wind again) can turn. In these
mills the vertical driving shaft that carries the power from the sails to
the stones and other machinery (hoists, etc.—for all hoisting is done

by wind-power) has to be dead-central so that the crown wheel on the axis of the sail shaft can revolve around it as the cap rotates.

Lime Kilns are fairly common, both in limestone or chalk areas and away from them. They are conical-shaped structures of brick or stone, with a big hopper in the top for holding the raw stone and a hearth beneath for the fire which was latterly of coal or anthracite although in times gone by wood was used (I have used wood in Africa). Lime was fired for two purposes: mortar, plaster and white-wash for building and for putting on the land. The reason why kilns are found in districts where there is no limestone is that it was easier (and pleasanter!) to carry raw limestone plus coal or anthracite than to carry quick or slaked lime. Lime when burnt turns to quicklime which is dangerous and corrosive. When it is slaked with water, or left to weather, it is hydrated lime—a fine powder, generally wet and puddingy, and very nasty to shovel out of the hold of a ship. Thus all around the coasts of Wales, Scotland and Ireland, and much of England, there are old lime kilns in most parts. Both stone and coal were brought in sailing ships, the lime burnt, and farmers would come down from the hinterland in their carts to carry away the lime. Nowadays burning is done in large kilns at a few quarries and any-way much of the limestone is ground and not burnt at all.

Religious Buildings. Stonehenge was probably built between 1900 and 1400 B.C., and certainly for Neolithic men in Britain, and sub-sequently for Bronze Age men it must have constituted their cathedral, or very holy place. It was in the Bronze Age (the Beaker Period, around 1700 B.C.) that the bluestones were transported from the Preseli Mountains in Pembrokeshire. Since they weigh some forty tons each and the Preselis are some two hundred miles away this will be seen as quite a feat. The Preseli region is peppered with stone

circles, *cromlechau* hut circles and barrows, and must have been a place of great importance in Neolithic and Bronze Age times, so holy that it was thought desirable to carry its stones this enormous distance to set up in a new, and more central, place.

Cromlechau (plural of *cromlech*) date from about 2000 B.C. They consist of one big stone balanced on top of three others. There are several in Cornwall and Pembrokeshire, but you get them as far north as the Orkneys and as far south as North Africa. They were probably the cores of earth mounds which have since washed away. Like many prehistoric monuments in our country they are said to have been tombs only because burials have been found in them. Possibly archaeologists of future ages will say that Westminster Abbey was a burial place only because burials will be found in it, and personally I have no doubt that *cromlechau*, and stone circles, and 'standing stones' or monoliths, were places of worship as well as tombs. The Druids were inclined to favour sacred groves instead of temples, but the foundations of pre-Christian Celtic temples have been discovered—a good one at Farley Heath and one at Maiden Castle in Dorset. In a few places, such as Caerwent and Silchester, Roman Christian chapels have been discovered, and one or two pre-Christian Roman temples such as the temple to Claudius at Colchester, two temples at St Albans, and Mithraic temples such as the one at Carrawburgh on Hadrian's Wall.

There are many buildings of Celtic Christianity about: *cashels* in Ireland, *keills* on the Isle of Man, *cils* in Wales. *Cil* means a monk's or hermit's cell, and most places with the prefix *cil* (Cilgerran) derive from this. The pattern of Celtic Christianity was a small and humble church, with a circular wall round it (the Welsh *llan* was the word used to describe these holy circular enclosures—hence the myriad Welsh place-names beginning with *Llan* followed by the name of a saint. The word for church in Welsh was taken from the Latin— *eglwys*). Beside the church would be cells for individual monks or nuns. An exact parallel can be found in present-day Ethiopia, where the graves of the faithful cluster *outside* the circular wall.

The death knell of Celtic Christianity was sounded at the Synod of Whitby (A.D. 664) at which the far more centralized and authoritarian Roman Christianity triumphed, men and women were segregated in religious houses and women given a secondary role in religion (many mixed-sex monasteries in Celtic times were governed by women, and this tradition lingered on a century or two in some places), monasteries became larger and life in them more organized. Churches also became larger and stone began to take the place of wood. There is plenty of 'Saxon' church building still to be found in England—generally in places which did not enjoy great prosperity in later ages and so little rebuilding was done. Saxon work can be recognized by such things as 'long and short work' in the corners— that is alternate horizontal and vertical stones making up the corners, very narrow slit windows with two slanting stones coming together at the top, narrow windows divided in half by a circular stone pillar in the middle and sometimes with a round arch at the top, occasionally round arched tower arches or doors, but having a quite different look about them from the round Norman arches. There is something very striking and primitive about Saxon architecture and it is immediately recognizable.

The Normans brought massive round pillars supporting the round Roman arch, often with rich carved decoration such as the very common 'dog-tooth' motif. In Early English times (beginning very

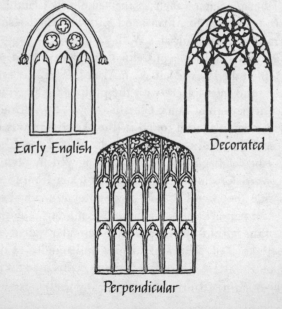

Early English

Decorated

Perpendicular

roughly about 1200) pointed arches came in, narrow lancet windows with pointed arched tops, clusters of smaller pillars around a central one—the smaller ones often of Purbeck Marble (a late Jurassic metamorphosed limestone) and the graceful vaults made possible by supporting vaulted roofs with pointed arches instead of round ones.

By 1300, windows were getting wider and were being filled in with the lush stone tracery of the Decorated Period. Marvellously elaborate stone carving is typical of this period—and it has a vigour and command of the medium never surpassed before or since. About 1400 (these dates are completely arbitrary of course, one 'period' merged gradually into another and at different speeds in different areas so if you give or take fifty years it is not too much), the Perpendicular Period took over with its much wider windows, characterized by perpendicular shafts of stone running straight from the top to the bottom, also pointed windows, of course, and much smaller spaces of wall between the windows so that in later Perpendicular country churches the wall seems to be mostly of glass. The great Suffolk and Norfolk 'wool churches' (churches rebuilt with the money that the woollen industry brought in in the fifteenth century) are fine examples of this. Lavenham, Southwold, Long Melford, all in Suffolk, are fine examples out of very many.

At the Reformation, Gothic (the pointed arch) gave way at last to the Classical Revival: a copying of Classical Greek and Roman styles. The round arch came back, the round-arch vault, Classical orders such as Doric, Ionian and Corinthian, and all the rest of it. This did not affect country churches much: lack of prosperity—or was it lack of piety?—in the villages precluded the pulling down of many of the fine medieval churches and replacing them with Classical. Also, soon after the Reformation the great Wesleyan movement swept the country, together with other Nonconformist sects, and most of the religious ardour of the country was turned into building fanes of quite a different character: Wesleyan, Methodist, Quaker, Baptist and many other kinds of 'meeting houses' and chapels, Classical in inspiration but unadorned and simple, although in Wales particularly there are some fine ones—austere and restrained maybe, but beautifully proportioned and magnificently built of dressed stone.

Military Buildings. In the Iron Age many great forts were built, often on promontories or on hill or mountain tops, defended by multiple walls and ditches which when in use were surmounted by wooden palisades. The walls as a rule enclosed many acres, on which a tribe could live with all its cattle until the enemy got tired and went away. The Romans stormed and destroyed many such forts when they conquered Britain. There were also long straight fortifications such as Devil's Dyke in Cambridgeshire, which, in common with all such linear defences down through the ages, could easily be stormed and breached. In Danish and Saxon times many such linear defences were built, such as Offa's Dyke which cuts England off from Wales.

The Romans built massive masonry forts, many of which survive, such as Portchester, Burgh Castle in Norfolk or Pevensey in Sussex, and these were so well made that, a thousand years after some of them were built, they were still good enough to be taken over by the conquering Normans.

The Normans built great keeps inside the Roman walls, or out in the country, at first throwing up steep-sided earth mounds called mottes and building wooden palisades on top of them—then surrounding the mottes with baileys, or fenced enclosures big enough for an army to live in with their horses, while the motte, or citadel, was kept as a last defence. Mottes soon had strong round keeps built on them which then gave way to square ones—but these gave way to round ones again as it was found that corners were too easily undermined and collapsed. The bailey walls were built of stone and fighting towers appeared in them—from which enfilading fire could be directed on an enemy attacking the walls. Later, under the influence of Saracen castles seen during the Crusades, keeps began to disappear and all the effort and material were put into the outer wall, which became very strong, and the castle itself. Then, with the coming of an effective cannon, the castle became impotent, and the feudal power that built it too.

Post-medieval fortification is a subject of great complexity and we cannot consider it in this book.

Chapter 5

———————— ⚜ ————————

Grass, the Forgiveness of Nature

We have dealt with the history of crops in the second chapter, so now let us consider the crops that we can actually see about our countryside today.

Grass, which in farming terms means grass-and-clover, is and always has been the most important and widespread crop we grow. It covers by far the biggest area of our farming land and is absolutely ubiquitous—you find it from the tops of the mountains down to the salt marshes of the sea. The herbivorous animals which form by far the greatest part of our domestic stock are by definition grass-eaters. Grass has been called 'the forgiveness of nature', for it heals the scars that we make in our greed and urgency. So long as land is under grass it is safe. It will not erode and wash away and, provided large crops of grass are not removed from it year after year in the form of hay or silage, it will steadily increase in fertility.

Grassland can roughly be divided into two categories—permanent pasture and ley. Ley means land that has been ploughed up and re-seeded to grass-and-clover or just grass. You can have a one-year ley or anything over. If you leave it long enough it becomes permanent pasture again, but many organic farmers nowadays use six-year leys. The rationale of it all is this: if you keep land permanently under the plough (i.e. plough it once or more a year) and grow arable crops off it every year it decreases in fertility unless you put plenty of manure of one kind or another on it, which is expensive. Further, it deteriorates in texture owing to the decay and non-replacement of humus. Humus is the word given to decaying organic matter in the soil and

87

it has manifold beneficial effects: it lightens and makes heavy land more friable, it makes light land 'heavier'—that is, it binds it and gives it the advantages of heavy land—it helps draining and aeration, it feeds and encourages nitrogen-fixing bacteria and earthworms which are highly beneficial in bringing up useful non-organic elements from the subsoil; it is essential for the health of the soil, the plants that grow on it and the animals (such as ourselves) that live on the plants. It is possible, as many agribusinessmen have found in the last two decades, to grow crops in humus-deficient land, but this can only be done by massive and ever-increasing applications of artificial fertilizer and, more important, of doses of fungicide, pesticide, selective weed sprays and chemicals that kill viruses and bacteria. It is nothing, nowadays, for such agribusinessmen to spray a crop of wheat six times during its growth—and *still* not hit the two tons an acre that many a good old-fashioned farmer got in days gone by with no chemicals at all. (The old-fashioned farmer had *men* though, which is the one thing the agribusinessman hasn't got many of.)

So good farmers do, and always have, practised the method of laying their arable land down to leys (the word *ley* comes from an Anglo-Saxon word meaning grass field) from time to time, to 'rest' the soil, build up the humus content, and build up the natural nitrogen by allowing the nitrogen-fixing bacteria to get to work—particularly the ones that live in symbiosis with the clovers.

There are two usual ways of laying down a ley. One is direct re-seeding—that is broadcasting (i.e. scattering) the seed on ploughed and harrowed land either in the spring (generally mid-April), and harrowing it in lightly so the birds don't get it all, or sowing it in the same way in the autumn, and the other method is sowing it with a 'nurse crop'. This may be Spring Corn (wheat, barley or oats) or some cruciferous crop like rape. The system is to drill your corn seed, or broadcast it (probably broadcast it if it is rape seed) and then broadcast the grass-and-clover seed on top and harrow it in and roll it well. The two crops grow together and when the corn is harvested, or the rape grazed off by cows or sheep in the late summer, the grass-and-clover is left. The advantage of this method is that time is not wasted, for you are getting a crop of corn or rape while the grass-clover is growing. The disadvantage is that you don't get quite such a good crop of either as you would with one alone, and therefore many farmers direct re-seed. This can be done in either spring or summer, on land ploughed and well worked down with the harrow or rotavator, either by broadcasting or by drilling with a special grass drill.

As for the species of grasses and clovers in the leys, these are few but there are many strains and varieties and plant breeders (notably at Aberystwyth) are constantly breeding new ones. The species (of which there are illustrations in this book) are, very broadly, of grasses:

Italian Ryegrass. This is an annual, that is it is only supposed to last a year and then must grow from seed again. It does in fact last

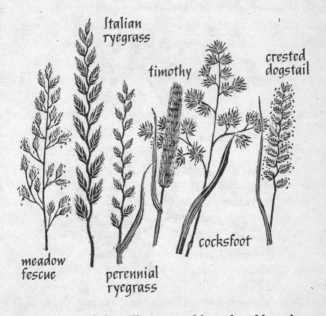

two or three years, and then dies out and is replaced by other grasses. It is much used for one-year leys and has the advantage that it gives an 'early bite'—i.e. it grows fast early in the year to feed stock when grass is very short (in the 'hungry gap' in fact). It has a very high yield and responds well to large dressings of nitrogenous fertilizer.

Perennial Ryegrass. This is by far the most important of our grasses from a farming point of view, and ryegrass pasture makes up about a quarter of the land in England and Wales under grass or rough grazing.

Timothy. Good for moister land. Gives a later bite in the spring than ryegrass and thus extends its grazing season.

Cocksfoot. Hardy and drought-resistant but not very palatable. Will dominate a pasture if not grazed fairly hard. Better for store cattle grazing than for fattening or milk production.

Meadow Fescue. Very palatable and not very aggressive in a pasture. Good on downland or the Cotswolds and other well-drained hills and makes up a large part of permanent pastures in such places.

Crested Dogstail. Good on upland or mountain pasture.

As for clovers, the ones usually sown in seed mixtures are:

White Clover, or New Zealand White Clover.

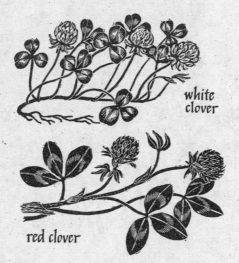

white clover

red clover

Wild White Clover. A most valuable creeping clover that spreads widely through a pasture.

Red Clover. A bold high-yielding clover, but can get clover sickness.

Alsike Clover. Good on damp, acid land, and is resistant to clover sickness which may knock out red clover.

There are other legumes such as *Sainfoin, Trefoil* and *Lucerne* (*Alfalfa* in America), which are sometimes sown by farmers. Lucerne

90

is very valuable in dry soils, being extremely drought-resistant because it sends its roots down to unbelievable depths if it can. It is very high-yielding, and three cuts a year in England are not uncommon and I have seen *eight* cuts in a year on irrigated lucerne in South Africa.

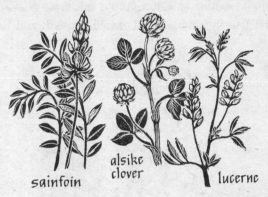

sainfoin   alsike clover   lucerne

Sensible farmers often add herb seeds to a permanent pasture mixture, such as Chicory, Burnet, Plantain, Yarrow and Sheep's Parsley. These send their roots deep down and bring valuable minerals up from the subsoil.

Typical seed mixtures contain a variety of grasses and clovers and sometimes herbs. As one example of thousands here is a mixture advocated by Professor M. McG. Cooper, a great grassland expert, for re-seeding hill pasture (quantities per acre):

>5 lb Danish Italian ryegrass
>12 lb S 23 or Kent ryegrass
>5 lb S 143 cocksfoot
>4 lb S 48 timothy
>2 lb crested dogtail
>1½ lb NZ or S 100 white clover
>1 lb Alsike clover
>½ lb wild white clover

Such symbols as 'S 23' denote the variety of the grass or clover concerned. There are a great many of such varieties, therefore the possible combinations of grass-and-clover seed mixtures are endless.

Every different soil and every different use calls for a different mixture, and the townsman who dismisses the farmer as a simple chap might just consider this.

It is strange, but convenient, that hard grazing (up to a point) encourages the better grasses at the expense of the worse ones. Thus ryegrass, wild white clover and the meadow grasses (*Poa* spp.) flourish on heavily trodden and grazed ground, and they are good

Yorkshire
fog

common bent

grazing plants, while bents (*Agrostis* spp.) fescues (*Fescues* spp.), Yorkshire fog (*Holcus lanatus*) flourish in less trodden and grazed areas and even rougher and less palatable and nutritious grasses on even less disturbed ground.

As for the care the farmer has to give to pasture: liming, slagging (phosphate addition) and potash addition all encourage the clovers at the expense of the grasses. Nitrogen addition encourages the grasses at the expense of the clovers, because it removes from the clovers their great advantage—that, like all legumes, they harbour nitrogen-fixing bacteria in nodules on their roots. Thus farmers know that to apply a little nitrogen to pastures is a complete waste: you merely replace the nitrogen that the clovers *would* have fixed for themselves with bought nitrogen. So to benefit from nitrogen application you must put heavy dressings on or none at all. The best dressing for pasture is in fact farmyard manure, because this is high in phosphate and potash and not too high in nitrogen; it always encourages the clovers and further encourages a pasture with *bottom* to it— that is a dense thick sward. But very heavy crops of rather unnutritious cloverless grass can be obtained by heavy applications of nitrogen.

Hard grazing encourages the clovers at the expense of the grasses, and the lighter grasses at the expense of the coarse cocksfoot. Continuous hard grazing weakens the pasture because it does not allow the roots of the plants to develop: thus intermittent grazing is better.

Strip grazing behind the electric fence is much practised by intensive cow farmers. The cows are allowed access to another narrow strip every day, and often the strip is *back-fenced* to prevent the cows going back to pasture already grazed over. The advantage is that the pasture is rested for a long period, which allows good root development and does it good, then grazed right down which does it good too. The cows are always on fresh clean grass and they leave their worm-infested droppings behind them. By the time the cycle goes round and they return to that strip the hope is that the worms will have died.

Zero-grazing is the process of keeping cows indoors all the time, cutting fresh grass for them with a forage harvester, and carting their dung back to the land in liquid form and spraying it on the pasture. I can see few advantages to it but it is practised by farmers who like to feel they have complete control over all natural processes no matter what this costs in the form of oil-derived power.

Paddock grazing is the cutting up of a farm into small paddocks by permanent fences and allowing the cows to graze each paddock for a limited period and then moving on to the next. It has all the advantages of strip grazing but is less work. It is poignant that farmers, having bulldozed out all the old beautiful hedges and stone walls on their farms in the interest of 'modernity', have now discovered that they were there for a purpose and are having to replace them by artificial fences in the interest of yet more 'modernity'. Maybe they should have left them there in the first place.

Mountain grazing is, or can be, a very high skill, and mountain pastures can be enormously improved by good treatment. Of course if you can spend the sort of money (or do the labour) to get lime on to them (they are nearly all acid—even the Millstone Grit mountains which *are* limestone), slag and drain them, and even go further and plough parts of them up and re-seed them, you can get very good pasture indeed. Subdividing with fences too can help a lot, because then you can rest certain portions and heavily graze others. Concentrated grazing forces stock to eat out the coarse and unpalatable grasses and scrub. You can kill bracken (the curse of hill land) by concentrating cattle on it in the early summer for example.

It has been estimated that we could double the production of meat in this country by improving hill and mountain grazing, but while the townsman expects his food nearly free this will never happen. At present hill and mountain grazing is going backwards fast.

As for the harvesting of grass, in so far as this is not done by grazing animals themselves, it was done originally by sickles (probably the flint-toothed sickles of Paleolithic Man), then by scythes. A man can scythe an acre a day but he has to be a very good man. A man can, in theory, *mow* (this is the old word meaning cut with a scythe) over two acres of wheat in a ten-hour day and up to four of barley and oats, but I believe an acre a day was far more common.

From 1780 on, many machines for the cutting of both grass and corn were invented. John Common of Northumberland built quite a

94

modern-looking reaper in 1812 but it didn't catch on. Patrick Bell of Forfarshire made a reaper in 1826 which was certainly the prototype of all subsequent ones. Some of his reapers were sent to America where, up to that date, no mechanical reaper had been invented. But America soon outstripped England, and Cyrus McCormick made a greatly improved version in 1834.

Nowadays most grass in Britain is cut with a simple mower attachment that fixes on to the side of a tractor, and is in the form of a reciprocating toothed knife working inside slotted fingers and thus producing a scissor action. Rotary grass cutters are coming into vogue now though: generally a series of round discs with sharpened edges which revolve at high speed and cut the grass. And most silage is cut by forage harvesters. These may have rotary cutters or they may have a horizontal drum with numerous short chains hanging from it and a blade swinging on each chain. The blades cut the grass off and it is blown by a fan up a spout and into an accompanying hopper.

To make hay the cut grass must be turned, fluffed up, protected if necessary from the rain, and carried to safety as soon as possible.

Right up to the Second World War much hay was 'made' (a word used by the countryman to mean, in this connection, dried) by turning it with wooden hay rakes, by hand, and with pitchforks (called *pikels* in some parts). The horse-rake was then generally brought into play to gather the dried hay into larger windrows (a windrow is a long ridge of grass or hay), then it was *cocked* with pitch forks, which means put into round-topped heaps that still allowed the wind to get through it to some extent but shed most of the rain. In these cocks it was fairly safe for a short period at least: while lying about on the ground it was constantly at risk. If the grass was still too green when it was put in the cock, perhaps prematurely because of threatening rain, then on the first fine day the cocks would have to be broken up and the grass scattered about in the sun and wind to go on drying again. On a threat of further rain it would be all hands into the field to rush the stuff into cocks again.

Finally well-dried, the hay was loaded, loose as it was, on to carts or wagons. With great skill enormous loads were loaded onto the long ship-like wagons—an older and more skilled man, the *loader*, standing up on top of the swaying load to distribute and consolidate the forkfuls that the *pitchers* were heaving up to him from below. A cry of 'Ho' tight!' from the senior pitcher was a sign both for the loader to shove his fork into the load to support himself and brace himself for the swaying and for the horse to move forward to the next cock. '*Whoa*! Ho'd you on now!' the pitcher would cry angrily to the horse if the latter forgot to stop at the next cock by himself. Finally, when the load seemed to tower upwards towards the sky, a pitcher would fling a light rope right over it from corner to corner, the loader—often an old man in his seventies—would swing himself down to the ground by it, and its free end would be hove down taut by a special knot known as 'the wagoner's knot' (which is still used, by the way, by lorry drivers).

Back in the stackyard a team of skilled men (the most skilled of all would work on top of the stack, perhaps with two assistants) would carefully stack the hay. The walls of the stack would have to sway outwards up as far as the eaves, then—'Time to *pull in*' the chief stacker would say and the stack would come in at a steep angle until the ridge was reached, or, in the case of a round stack, a point. The kind of judgement needed to lay out the foundations of a big stack to accommodate *exactly* the produce of a ten-acre field, say, and to know *exactly* when to start 'pulling in' so as to come to the top at the right angle, and not have a pitchforkful of hay left over, nor to have to borrow hay from another field to fill up, is comparable to the judgement needed to broadcast a field of wheat seed. And yet I have seen, and many times, the last forkful of hay from a field passed up from the unloader to the man in the *bull-hole* (a hole left at the eaves in which a man could stand in order to be able to pass the hay up from the unloader way down on the wagon to the stacker right up on top of the stack) for him to tread it down underneath his feet and for it to fill exactly the space left to be filled. One forkful more would have been too many and one less would not have been enough, and that would have been in a stack weighing perhaps twenty tons. Such quite astonishing feats of accurate prediction (it must be remembered that tonnage of hay from a field varied greatly from year to year) used to make me wonder if old farm workers did not have some instinct that was almost supernatural!

The stacks would be left then until a man and a boy were free from other pressing work and then thatched thinly with wheat straw. Once the stacks were thatched there was no further concern about the hay: it could be left for three or four years if necessary without deteriorating.

Nowadays there are many different machines—'wooflers', tedders and turners—to fling the grass about to dry it or gather it up into windrows, and then there is the ubiquitous *pick-up baler* to come behind it all and bale it. The baler, pulled by a tractor generally, crawls along like some hungry monster, making that rhythmical *thump—thump* as its heavy ram pounds the hay into a form, and excretes heavy solid bales behind it, tightly tied with twine. The advantage of baling is that it enormously reduces the time needed to cart a field of hay, and also, later in the winter when this stored grass is being used, it makes the feeding of stock much easier. A man can carry a bale on his back, cut the twines and feed out the compressed hay quite easily. Loose-stacked hay had to be cut with the huge blade of a *hay knife*, and this used to be very hard work indeed.

There are, as one would imagine there would be, various devices for elevating the bales from the field on to the tractor-drawn trailers that carry them to the barn. But by and large the coming of the hay bale has not lightened the work of the individual hay-maker. It has merely made it possible to carry hay with fewer people. Most hay bales are still slung up to the load by hand—and to do this all day, with bales weighing half a hundredweight, soon finds the weak places in you!

Chapter 6

The Arable Land

'Tis strange that no Author should have written fully on
the Fabric of Ploughs! Men of the greatest Learning have
spent their Time in contriving Instruments to measure the
immense Distances of Stars, and in finding out the Dimen-
sions, and even Weight, of the Planets: they think it is more
eligible to study the Art of ploughing the Sea with Ships
than of tilling the Land with Ploughs: they bestow the
utmost of their skill learnedly, to pervert the natural use of
all the Elements for Destruction of their own Species, by
the Bloody Art of War. Some waste their whole lives in
studying how to arm Death with new Engines of Horror and
inventing an infinite Variety of Slaughter; but think it
beneath Men of Learning (who only are capable of doing it)
to employ their learned Labours in the Invention of new . . .
Instruments for increasing of Bread.

Jethro Tull, 1731

When the first man (or more probably woman) stuck a gemsbok horn
into the hard soil of Africa, and levered out the wild plants that were
already growing there, and sprinkled some grass seed stolen from the
ants on to the disturbed ground, arable agriculture had begun. This
man or woman, whoever it was, made the greatest invention that
mankind has ever made or ever will make.

If you sprinkle seeds on old grassland, or throw them in a wood, all
that happens is that the birds eat them. To get them to grow you

must destroy or suppress the existing wild vegetation. We do this nowadays by ploughing—a process which inverts the top layer of the soil and thus buries the wild vegetation that is growing. Into the exposed earth, or on its surface, we then place our seed.

Large areas of the earth are still tilled with the digging stick. A superior tool to this is also still widespread—the hoe, or mattock. At ceremonial dances in the Upper Zambesi country the women carry miniature ornamental mattocks, while the men carry miniature axes. The role of man in such countries is to fell and burn the forest trees: of woman to hoe or mattock the ground and plant the seed.

As soon as man had harnessed the first animal (and I believe that was man and not woman) it was easy to pull a sharpened digging stick through the ground by animal power, and ploughing like this can be seen in many parts of the tropics. The little plough that an Indian *ryot* can carry to the field on his shoulder, to be pulled by two bullocks or buffaloes, is an extension of this.

The Saxons, as we have seen, used a mould-board plough much like the ploughs we have today. Essentially their plough, and ours, consisted of a *coulter*, which is a vertical blade going down into the soil to make the vertical cut of the furrow, a *share*, which is a broad pointed blade which goes under the ground and makes the horizontal cut, and the *mould-board* or *breast*, which is a curving plate, of wood or iron or steel, which comes behind the share and turns or inverts the slice that has been cut by the other two pieces. That is a plough and one is tempted to think always will be. Certainly it is hard to think of anything better. In tropical and sub-tropical countries, true, the *disc plough* is much used and I often wonder why it isn't in this country under certain circumstances. A multiple disc plough is a number of steel discs, set in a line at an angle to the line of progression, each disc set at an angle also and heavily *dished* so that its action is to cut into and then invert the soil. The sharp cutting edges of the revolving discs will cut through surface rubbish and trash that would stifle a mould-board plough. They break the soil up as they turn it, and do not leave the polished continuous surface of the inverted furrow so beloved of British ploughmen. I have been responsible for the ploughing of hundreds of acres with three-furrow disc ploughs pulled by teams (or 'spans') of ten oxen, and a very good job they did too. Maybe one day a British farmer will have the courage to try a disc plough.

The Gauls when they came to Britain brought a wheeled plough, and most horse-drawn ploughs in Britain now are wheeled, but you do still see *swing ploughs* and I have used them. They have no wheels and do a very good job—but only in the hands of a very good ploughman (which I was not!).

Ploughs began to be improved very seriously in the eighteenth century. In 1705, one of the first of the engineering Ransome family applied for a patent to make shares of cast iron, instead of wrought iron as they had been before. A wrought-iron share had to be taken constantly to the blacksmith to be resharpened. It was the Ransomes who designed the fine 'Rutland Plough' which came out in 1834, and they are still turning out good ploughs. The Rutland had a big wheel and a small wheel—the big one to go in the furrow and the small one on the unploughed land. The heavy ploughs used in the clay soils of the Weald of Kent and Sussex hung in a large 'gallows': a sort of carriage all of its own in which the beam of the plough was suspended.

By about 1850 steam came into ploughing—a gang of ploughs being dragged back and forth across the field by a traction engine with a big windlass drum underneath it and an endless wire rope going round a pulley at the far side of the field. This contraption was still in use up to 1940 but I doubt if one is in commercial use now. An internal combustion tractor won a prize at the Royal Show at Manchester in 1897, and in the First World War tractors became relatively common. By the start of the Second World War horses were still predominant, however, and it was that war which forced the pace of mechanization on: farmers had to farm with little labour because the men who should have been working the land were in the forces.

The first practicable tractor-hauled plough came out in 1904. A man had to sit on it to pull the lever that lifted the shares out of the ground at headlands so the thing could turn. In 1919 a device came in by which the tractor driver could lift the shares out by pulling a cord attached to a lever. Shortly before the Second World War Harry Ferguson invented the 'three-point linkage' system, which revolutionized tractor work and incidentally saved what were left of the hedges of England. A plough (or any other device) used with this system need have no wheels of its own and can be lifted clear out of the ground by the simple action of a lever by the driver. Thus the plough can be backed right into the hedge and there is no need to leave a wide headland. Thus it was no longer so urgent to grub out hedges. This invention is now widespread over the world.

A variety of implements are used to get a seed-bed after ploughing. The *harrow* is very ancient: probably it started as a bunch of thorn bushes dragged over the ground with a weight on top of them, then a wooden framework with wooden pegs sticking downwards to scarify the soil, then iron took the place of wood, then the spring-tine harrow came in the better to pulverize the clods, the *roller* to crush clods and consolidate the soil, the *disc harrow* which is just a series of small sharp discs that cut up the surface, the *cultivator*, which has strong tines which are dragged deep through the soil—now by tractors but once by a team of horses—the *rotavator* which has a revolving drum with tines on it driven from the engine of the tractor and which can do the work of a plough and achieve a seed-bed in one.

The art of 'getting a seed-bed', particularly in heavy land, is a fine one. It is very easy to 'puddle' such land and make it turn into hard unbreakable clods. The practice of ploughing heavy land up and leaving it in the furrow through the winter for 'the frost to get at it' was dear to the hearts of Englishmen for generations but is now suspect. There is a growing school which says it is better to sow a crop of sainfoin or clover or some other legume and plough that in in the spring, thus increasing the humus and nitrogen supply in the soil and avoiding the leaving of broken-up land bare all winter, when the rains undoubtedly wash much of the goodness out of it.

There is a new culture which does without the plough altogether, and that is the spraying of land with toxic chemicals such as *paraquat* which kill all vegetation. It is then possible to drill seed direct into the sterilized soil. The *paraquat* becomes less lethal when it falls to the soil, although what effect such constant dosing with lethal chemicals has on soil life is not known and can only be guessed at.

The subsequent weeding of crops can be done by hand or with

the hand-hoe, the horse-hoe, the tractor-hoe, or by chemicals. Corn is not generally weeded in Britain—if the land into which it is drilled is sufficiently *clean*, which means in this context weed-free, the corn will grow quickly and beat the weeds. All *row crops*, however—crops drilled in rows wide enough apart to let the hoe through—have to be weeded. Indeed part of the purpose of growing them is so they *can* be weeded—and the land thus cleaned for subsequent corn crops. Nowadays there is a huge battery of toxic chemicals to take the place of the hoe: some crops of corn are sprayed as many as seven times during their growth with chemicals of one sort or another, some to kill weeds, some to try to prevent disease.

As for fertilizing or feeding the land, the time-honoured *muck cart* is now in eclipse, although there are still some about. Thirty years ago good farmers fattened large herds of bullocks in their sheds during the winter, bedding them comfortably on plenty of clean straw, and the straw was turned to compost by the dung and treading of the animals, and hundreds of tons of it were carted out onto the land the subsequent summer and winter. Such muck as is still spread is spread by the *muck-spreader*, or even sprayed as 'slurry'.

Chilean nitrate started coming into this country in 1835, and it was the start of a new agricultural revolution. It was the accumulated droppings of sea birds in ancient times in a dry climate and was very rich in nitrogen. Peruvian guano eked it out—the fresh droppings of living sea birds. A great fleet of square-rigged ships was employed carrying millions of tons of this stuff around Cape Horn to Europe. But in 1803 a German chemist, Justus von Leibig, found out how to synthesize soluble nitrate (i.e. nitrogen in a form that plants can use) from the air by the use of electricity. Now vast amounts of nitrogenous chemicals with such names as Sulphate of Ammonia, Nitram, Nitrochalk, Nitrosax and Nitro are used by farmers each year, in ever-increasing doses made necessary by the increasing debilitation of the soil. More and more straw is burnt, because the farm animals have been divorced from the soil and in any case there are cheaper ways of keeping animals than on straw, all weeds are shrivelled up with chemicals, and thus no vegetable or animal waste is returned to the soil. Soluble nitrogen takes the place of it though—and the other elements that plants must have: phosphate and potash. Nearly all the artificial fertilizers at present used in this country come from abroad, but when the vast potash deposits found four thousand feet down under the Cleveland National Park in north Yorkshire, in the deposits left by the dying Zechstein Sea, come on flow, at least Britain will be self-sufficient in one element: potassium. Nitrogen, though, is at present extracted from the air by the expenditure of enormous amounts of power, and if power becomes scarce, soluble nitrogen will too. It already has recently with the rise in the price of oil. Maybe we will one day have to go back to the muck cart again, and *leys* of grass and clover to put 'heart' back into the land. Plenty of farmers in Cobbett's day, the early 1800s, used to achieve two tons of wheat an acre with no chemicals at all, and plenty of farmers in our day, with all these chemicals, don't achieve it. If the energy *input-output* ratio is considered, though, there is no comparison between the 'efficiency' of the old kind of animal-based husbandry and the new chemical-based. It has been calculated that it takes six calories of energy in the form of oil, chemicals and fertilizers to produce one calorie of energy in the form of wheat on modern monocultural wheat farms. Still, a small but growing group of farmers in this country is experimenting with the old methods—and, more excitingly, with new methods of their own —with the object of eliminating the use of such enormous quantities of oil-derived power and chemicals from agriculture.

Chapter 7

The Crops of Arable Land

Now for the crops of arable land—land which has been *ploughed* (or occasionally, in these days, sprayed with a herbicide in lieu of ploughing).

What is called *corn* in England (corn in the U.S.A. means maize only) is wheat, barley, oats and rye, and these are all grasses, but we consider them separately from the 'grasses' we have discussed above because we grow them primarily not to be grazed off by animals but to come to ripeness of grain so that we can harvest the grain itself. Nothing is simple in farming, and in fact all the corns are used for grazing as well as for grain production. This is done in two ways: by grazing off a 'winter-proud' crop of any winter-sown corn with sheep in the spring so as to set it back, cause it to *tiller* (that is to multiply its growing stalks) and produce a stronger crop, and also by simply growing a crop of any of the corns and grazing it off as one would grass and then ploughing the land up again. *Rye* is very often used for this purpose—in fact it is its chief use in Britain.

But by far the greater acreage of corn in this country is grown for grain, and the practice of grazing-off winter corn is very seldom seen any more.

Corn nowadays is sown, almost always in England and generally in Wales, Scotland and Ireland, with a drill. Only by eccentrics like the writer, or in remote parts of the Celtic countries is corn broadcast by hand in the manner made familiar by illustrators of the Bible. Hand-broadcasting requires more seed for the same result: say four bushels to the acre instead of three in the case of the drill, but done

104

properly and under good conditions it can give as good a result. A good *tilth* is prepared, by ploughing and then harrowing with a choice of a variety of implements, the seed is scattered by the sower's hand evenly over the field, then the field is harrowed again and preferably rolled as well. The reputation of the sower is made or broken by the appearance of the field when the corn comes up. A good sower can sow a twenty-acre field so that not even the area of the palm of a man's hand anywhere on the field is without a seed on it and no such area has more than three or four, and I have seen a neighbour sow a five-acre field at four bushels to the acre and have watched the final handful of seed land on the last tiny corner of the field at exactly the same density of sowing as the first handful in the opposite corner. This sort of skill is derived from more than just intelligence: there is a touch of genius in here somewhere.

Genius, however, is not needed to operate the modern seed drill. The invention of the seed drill is generally attributed to Jethro Tull. He published his book *The New Horse-houghing Husbandry* in 1731, and in it described a workable seed drill. His ideas had enormous influence on British agriculture and through that on the agriculture of the world, but in fact an effective seed drill with revolving cups to feed the seed into the chutes that took it into the ground had been made by an Italian, Locatelli, in 1670, and the Babylonians and Egyptians had manually operated seed drills (the seeds were dropped by hand down a pipe which fed them into the ground behind a plough) many centuries before Christ; and the Ethiopians use a seed drill working on this principle to this day.

Most corn in Britain is now harvested with the combine harvester, although you may still see, very rarely, a reaper-and-binder at work. If there is still a *reaper* working in the British Isles it is unknown to me.

Briefly, a reaper was a machine that cut the crop with a reciprocating knife and chucked it into little heaps, each the size of a sheaf. People (often women and children) followed the reaper, picked the bundles up, and tied them round the middle by a twist of a handful of the corn itself.

The reaper-and-binder—which came to be known as the binder *tout court* was a reaper with a cunning attachment for tying the sheaves up with string, and chucking the completed sheaf out of the side. This immediately reduced very drastically the labour required for harvesting and threw a lot of people out of work, and it also made women and children redundant in the harvest field, which spoiled a lot of the fun. When I was young the child's role in the harvest field was to chase the rabbits which bolted out of the shrinking

square of standing corn left in the middle of the field and to kill them with sticks, for rabbits were a pest then and were also very good eating; but the arrival of myxomatosis, which killed nearly all the rabbits, also killed this. Now the harvest field is a boring affair of huge machines, combine harvesters, which cut, thresh, winnow, and either bag the grain or blow it into a bulk tank, and are driven round and round by dusty and noise-deafened men, while other dusty and noise-deafened men drive back and forth the tractors which take the grain back to the barn, either in sack or bulk tanker but nowadays more and more in bulk tanker. If in bulk tanker it is tipped straight into a sump, and elevated by screw-elevator into a grain drier, artificially dried by the expenditure of considerable fuel, then transferred mechanically into bulk holders.

Reapers were always pulled by horses (for tractors didn't exist in the days of the reaper). Binders were first pulled by horses—often three big horses to pull a big binder with three more in reserve so that the teams could be changed round frequently as the horses became exhausted from this gruelling work—then by tractor, and latterly by tractor with P.T.O. (Power Take Off) drive. The first binders had their cutting and binding mechanism driven from the

106

ground wheels (i.e. the forward progression of the machine turned its wheels round and these drove the machinery). The P.T.O. binders had their machinery driven by a shaft from the engine of the tractor and were far more efficient.

The first combine harvesters were pulled by large teams of horses or mules in Canada and the United States. The combine harvester of today has its own diesel engine aboard which both drives it along and powers its intricate machinery. The threshed, winnowed and sieved grain is nearly always blown up a spout and into a tractor-drawn or self-propelled hopper which keeps pace beside the combine, or it can be stored in a tank in the combine and discharged into a hopper at intervals. The straw is chucked out at the back. Combines were a rarity in Britain right up to, and including, the Second

World War. Now they have almost completely taken over from binders. The reason for their early popularity in North America and late adoption in Britain was climate. In the dry Canadian summer the grain is bone-dry when it is harvested and can be taken straight to the huge grain elevators that dot the landscape of the wheat prairies and be pumped in to await shipment. In Europe, however, grain must generally be dried if cut with a combine, and this adds expense and complication. When cut with the binder it is 'stooked' in the field—that is the *sheaves* (bundles) are propped up against each other and left to dry. Barley dries fairly quickly thus, wheat a little longer and oats must be 'churched three times': that is it must stand in the stook for three Sundays before being carried. Stooks are also called, in different parts of the country, *shocks*, *hiles* or *traives*.

In England such binder-cut corn is generally carried straight from the stooks to the rickyard and stacked or ricked. In the wetter western areas it was (and occasionally still is—on the writer's farm for example) *mowed*. This *mow* is quite a different word from the *mow* that means to cut corn or grass. A *mow*, in this sense, is a pile of, say, fifty sheaves—thus far bigger than a stook which has only six or eight. First a filled circle of sheaves is set on the ground, ears upwards. Then a layer of sheaves ears downwards is built on top of them, starting from the middle, each sheaf bound to the one next door by a twist of its own straw which is pushed under the string or band of its neighbour. Thus the sheaves cannot slip. Layer after layer are put on in this way, each smaller than the one below, until the mow ends in a point or apex of about four sheaves with their ears upwards and waving in the breeze. A mow will shed rain, allow a certain amount of drying of the corn and straw inside it, and protect the corn until well into the winter: I have had corn in the mow until after Christmas. There is pressure though to clear the field long before then so as to be able to use the grazing. In that case the corn is carried from the mows either to the threshing machine or to the rickyard or to the Dutch barn if the lucky farmer has enough room in one. The many pubs called 'The Barley Mow' are named after this kind of mow. Carrying to the rickyard is by no means the end of the harvesting operation, however. For even when 'all is safely gathered in' and the corn is in the rick there is still plenty of work to do before we can eat it, feed it to the stock, or make beer of it.

First it must be threshed (the grain knocked out of the straw by some method) then it must be winnowed and cleaned. Threshing was done years ago by the flail, which is a simple tool made by joining a short stick to a long one by a flexible link of some sort. Eel skin was the traditional link in the eastern counties, leather or sometimes even twisted willow or hazel bonds elsewhere. The corn is laid on the floor and the stick brought down hard upon it in such a manner that the short stick is laid flat upon it. Other methods in other parts of the world involve driving animals round and round on the corn and straw so that their feet trample out the grain ('Muzzle not the ox which treadeth the grain'), and I have seen this done with mules, oxen, donkeys and water buffalo. In rice areas particularly, young men sometimes stamp the grain out with their bare feet, all standing holding on to a horizontal bar for support and, in Ceylon for example, singing lustily as they tread. Hauling a heavy wooden frame (sometimes set underneath with flints) over the corn is another method.

In 1636, an attempt was made in England to invent a threshing machine. This consisted of a number of flails whizzing round a drum. But it was not until 1786 that Andrew Meikle, of East Lothian, (whose father, James, had invented a winnower) invented a really successful *threshing drum*. This was a revolving drum with wooden pegs stuck into it and a *concave*, or concave-shaped grid half way round it. Corn shoved between the drum and the concave got threshed—i.e. the loosened grain fell through the bars of the concave and the threshed straw was pushed through to the other side. The modern drum is just this except that instead of wooden pegs there are steel bars. At first threshing drums were driven by horses walking around in a circle, or even by manpower, and many by water power (a few still are in Wales), then mostly by steam, and now the few stationary drums that remain are generally driven by a belt from the diesel tractor.

Refinements soon followed in the threshing machines, such as the *straw walker*, which had a number of parallel wooden girders, which moved alternately with a reciprocating movement to 'walk' the threshed straw away from the drum so that any grain still clinging to the straw would fall out, a *fan*, or *winnower*, which was a revolving fan to create a wind to blow the chaff away from the grain, and a whole series of reciprocating sieves some of which were large mesh to allow all the grain to go through but stop any bits of straw or chaff, others of which were smaller, in different sizes, to intercept the grain of different sizes and deliver it at separate spouts.

To work in a threshing gang in the steam days was an arduous, dusty, but joyful experience. Eight or nine men might be employed, many of them the regular travelling threshing gang—rough and tough men they were too, hard drinkers, hard workers, used to roughing it and sleeping in barns. They carried bicycles, very often, slung up on the 'drum' when they moved from farm to farm, the whole cavalcade moving at a stately pace: first the steam engine, then the great red-painted bicycle-hung drum itself, then a tall straw elevator used for carrying the straw away from the drum to the top of the straw stack. When working, the engine would be chuffing

109

away, blowing out smuts and smoke; the engineer, the most important man of all, busy with his oil can or coal shovel; the long belt whipping about and a danger to go near; the great drum humming loudly, and making growling noises as sheaf after sheaf was fed into it, its manifold sieves and shakers and walkers all rattling and clanging; men shouting to each other—mostly jokes and badinage—three men up on the corn-rick pitchforking down the sheaves; the most trusted old fellow standing over the deadly drum itself (if he fell in he would be quite literally turned to mincemeat for the 54-inch steel drum was revolving at five hundred revolutions per minute), carefully cutting the strings off the sheaves and feeding the corn in slowly so as not to choke the drum; the farmer and a helper or two on the ground at the back of the drum bagging up the corn from perhaps four chutes which delivered different sizes—and often weighing the heavy bags before tying them up; three more men high up on the straw stack with pitchforks trying to cope with the deluge of threshed straw being showered on them from the elevator; and you, if you were the *boy*, carrying huge but fairly light bags of *chaff* (husks) away from a horrible dusty hole underneath the machine to dump it into some shed, where it would wait to be mixed with the oats of the horses. This chaff-carrying job was abominably dusty—I have had plugs of dust an inch long sticking out of each nostril and masses of thistle prickles and other rubbish inside my sweaty clothes. But the fun and excitement of it all and the feeling that one was doing a man's job made up for it all. Also, you had the knowledge that you would not be 'boy' for ever—and supposing one day, when you were old and grey, you had the glory of being the man with the knife up on the threshing drum?

Now as to the different species of corn we grow, of course we must first consider *wheat*.

Wheat is the crop on which Western civilization is based, and has been based for several thousand years. It forms the main support of human life in most of Europe, North America (outside what used to be known as the 'corn and hog belt'—corn in this case being maize), North Africa, the Middle East, West Pakistan, Northern India (rice is hardly used in the Punjab and most of Uttar Pradesh), Northern China, Australia and the Western Cape of South Africa. It is the chief food crop anywhere, in fact, where the climate allows it to be grown and harvested satisfactorily. And would it be arrogant for a wheat-eater (man not bird) to say that the civilizations which have been built on it have tended to be superior ones?

Wheat is probably derived from two or three wild grasses, and selection over the ages, hybridization and mutation, has resulted in a

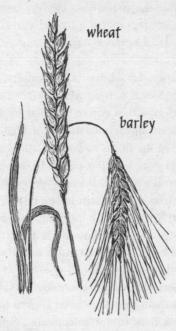

wheat

barley

large variety of basically similar strains. It is by and large self-fertilizing, which means that it breeds most of the time true to type, but it can be artificially inseminated from other individuals in the plant-breeding station and thus new breeds can be developed.

There are two main divisions of varieties: winter wheat and spring wheat. The former has to be sown in the autumn (say, in England, in September or October) and the latter in the spring—in England, March or April. The winter wheat thus germinates in the autumn, remains more or less dormant throughout the winter (it is an advantage if it can be protected by a nice covering of snow, but if not it is pretty frost-resistant), and then gets off to a flying start as soon as spring breaks out to be harvested in August or early September.

It tends to give heavier yields than spring wheat and most of the wheat planted in this country is winter wheat. When you see fields of tender green grass-like shoots on the heavier land of England in the winter time they may well be shoots of winter wheat. These shoots will be slightly darker in colour than barley, although not very different in shade from oats, but you can tell immature wheat from the others by the fact that wheat has no leaf horns. These are little horns that enfold the stem of the plant at the base of the leaves— like tiny horns. Barley has large stamens, and oats has stamens but they are very small.

The climatic range of wheat is enormous. Wheat grows in Russia, Siberia and Canada (spring wheat only of course) but the best wheat I ever saw in my life was that planted by Hottentots in their reserve at Franzfontein in the very north of Damaraland—well into the tropics and one of the hottest places in the world. This wheat of course was under irrigation. What wheat likes is rain when it wants it and drought when it wants it. It needs water in the early stages of its growth, is very drought-resistant in the middle and later periods, and to harvest it well you need a long hot dry spell. In Britain we very often have to put up without the latter. It likes *strong* land, that is, land with a high clay fraction, in other words fairly heavy. It does not yield well on sandy soil.

As for what wheat will yield—there are certain modern wheats, such as Maris Huntsman, that have been known to yield four tons an acre, and three tons now is not uncommon. Such yields, though, strike the writer as something in the nature of a stunt. It is merely a matter of developing a wheat that will respond to enormous levels of nitrate application and then providing them: the grower is not producing wheat from his soil but simply turning bought nitrogen, potassium and phosphorous into inferior wheat. The energy input-output ratio of such agriculture is appalling. Further the wheat has to be treated like a vegetable invalid: weed competition must be totally eliminated with pre-emergence and contact sprays and fungicides and insecticides in great quantities have to be deployed to destroy pests and diseases.

Two tons an acre is much more common, and can be achieved with ordinary wheats on good land with good treatment and no artificial fertilizers, chemical weed-killers, fungicides or pesticides at all. Late eighteenth-century and early nineteenth-century writers such as Arthur Young and Cobbett were constantly noting two-ton-an-acre in their travels. They took this as something good but not unusual in those days of High Farming. No chemicals were used (there weren't any) but enormous applications of farmyard manure kept up the high fertility of the land, plus the ploughed-in residues of nitrogen-fixing clovers, the bulk of humus-forming grasses, and the dunging and treading of sheep which were kept folded on turnips. I worked on a farm in Essex as a pupil when a boy where two tons of wheat to the acre was the almost invariable rule and where hardly any chemical fertilizer and no other chemicals were used. There were, though, a hundred bullocks fattened every year in yards on this hundred-acre farm, a herd of six breeding sows, the dung of five horses and a couple of hundred free-range hens. This was one of the last farms in Essex run on traditional High Farming lines. No fuel-oil was imported on to the farm for there were no tractors or other engines. The only thing that did come over our borders was a ton or two of linseed cake for what Mr Catt the farmer called 'its *kindling* effect' on the bullocks to give them a finish for the butcher in the last weeks of the fattening period. The input-output ratio of such a farm was simply marvellous—practically nothing came on but a great deal went off. But such farming is prodigal of *human labour*. There were seven of us working these hundred acres and we had to work in a way which no modern farm worker would tolerate. Today this farm is probably part of a thousand-acre agribusiness with possibly two tractor drivers working the whole lot.

But apart from the stunt members of the three-ton-and-over club (who are certainly costing the country far more in foreign exchange than they are saving by producing wheat) the average production of wheat per acre in Britain is still well below two tons an acre.

Wheat suffers from some spectacular diseases. The *Rusts* (Yellow, Brown and Black) cause great loss—in fact Black Rust has brought famine behind it and changed the course of history on many occasions. It has a secondary host—the Barberry Bush, and the Crusaders merrily brought this pernicious plant back from the Holy Land with them, thus bringing Black Rust too and causing great famines in

Europe. The story of the discovery of the connection between Black Rust and the Barberry in the seventeenth century by a French priest is fascinating. Certainly no Barberry Bush should be allowed to exist in any wheat-growing country for longer than it takes to find an axe and a box of matches.

Smut is also a very destructive disease, as is *Bunt*. Dressing of wheat seed in a fungicide kills the latter: the former can be prevented by using only clean seed. All these diseases only become damaging when wheat is grown too extensively; when plenty of other crops are grown besides wheat, so that wheat only occurs occasionally in the rotation, diseases are negligible.

Now for the vexed question of *hard wheat* versus *soft wheat*. Wheats grown in dry climates, like the summer climate of North America, tend to be hard. English wheats tend to be soft. All that these terms mean is that some wheats ('hard') have a high gluten content—others ('soft') low. Gluten in the flour causes it to retain gas better—in others words to blow up into large bubbles because of the carbon-dioxide given off by the yeast in the dough. This causes a 'lighter' loaf. The lightness due to large gas bubbles is, however, offset by the fact that 'hard' flour retains water better. Thus the weight lost by large bubbles is made up by water. Now obviously the best flour from a baker's point of view is the one which yields the most loaves per sack—and if he can sell plenty of carbon-dioxide and water in his loaves then he is happy. Therefore he prefers 'hard' flour. If you grow, grind and bake your own wheat, however, there is no advantage whatever in 'hard' wheat—in fact I should say, as one who does it, rather the reverse.

Wheat straw is good for bedding and good for thatching but useless as a feed.

Barley is interesting in that its protein content is quite different from that of wheat. It is not in the form of gluten (therefore barley bread does not rise very well—it is very *dense*) but is soluble, which is what makes that peculiar substance *barley-water* possible (for good or for ill). Barley is very high in starch, and therefore suitable for making beer. The process of making beer is that the starch of barley is converted into sugar (maltose) by the action of enzymes inside the grain, which get to work when the grain is germinated. This conversion of insoluble starch to soluble sugar is necessary before the plant can grow: energy is best stored in the form of starch but used in the form of sugar which can easily be transported about the plant. The maltster then germinates the seed—by keeping it wet and warm. When it begins to *shoot* (grow) he *kills* it by heating it in a kiln. This also dries it so that it will keep. Having kilned it he cracks it in a mill. The brewer takes the resulting *malt* as it is called, steeps it in hot water, which dissolves the sugar out of it, allows this water to cool and adds yeast to it. The yeast—a living organism—eats the sugar and turns it into alcohol.

The high starch content of barley also makes it a high-energy food for pigs and cattle. It is a good fattening food. The best of the barley grown in England is sold for malting, the rest of it for animal feed. Very little is consumed by humans except in the form of beer.

Barley, as we have seen, can be distinguished from wheat and oats in its very early stages by the fact that there are very large horns reaching around the stem at the base of its leaves. In the ear it is distinguishable by its long sharp whiskers emanating from the grains. It is cultivated much like wheat except that much more barley is planted in the spring than is wheat (although there are winter barleys), it likes a much finer seed-bed, it doesn't need such rich ground—in fact to get a good 'malting sample' you need fairly poor ground. It doesn't yield as much per acre as wheat. You are more likely to see barley growing in the west and Wales and Scotland than you are wheat: wheat does not like very wet summers and a wet harvest. Barley, for malting at least, must be cut dead ripe, and so the straw has little feed value although cattle will eat it and it is better than nothing. It is too brittle and generally too short for thatch and not too good for litter although that is where most of it ends up on farms where they do not burn it.

Oats were at one time more widely grown in Britain than either wheat or barley. When Doctor Johnson twitted Boswell by telling him that oats was the main food for people in Scotland but was only considered fit for horses in England, Boswell answered: 'Yes—you have better horses—we have better people', or words to that effect.

Oats will grow in a wetter climate than wheat or barley, tolerate acid soils, and grow at a high altitude. Cut slightly green with a binder or by scythe and then tied in sheaves, it can be fed to horses or cattle just like that—in the sheaf. The cattle eat it straw and all. Generally, though, it is threshed, either with stationary drum or with combine, and rolled before being fed to cattle or horses. It is without doubt the best food there is for horses, very good for cattle, of some use for poultry, of little value for pigs and as to whether you

rye

oats

think it a suitable food for human beings it depends whether you live north of the Border or not. Oat straw is excellent fodder for cattle or horses—nearly as good as hay.

Potatoes are generally grown in ridges, which are made by ridging ploughs mounted on tractors (or in a very few cases pulled by horses) so if you see a field ploughed up into a regular ridge-and-furrow pattern it will probably be potatoes (although, in the Black Fens of Lincolnshire, it may possibly be celery, but the ridges will be smaller).

The potato is not grown commercially from seed, but from *sets*, which are just potatoes, and so all the potatoes of one variety in the world are *one plant*. They are one individual that has just been divided and divided. To produce new varieties of potato it is necessary to grow plants from the actual seed which grows in the fruit of the potato (which resemble miniature tomatoes) and as potato fruit is self-fertilizing it is also necessary to emasculate the potato flower and fertilize the ovary with the pollen from the flower of another potato. When this is done many hundreds of times there is a possibility that a variety may be produced that is better than existing varieties. If this is thought to be so, the breeder arranges for his new variety to be multiplied by setting the actual potatoes from it—and if it proves a popular variety the original half-dozen or so potatoes on the first-ever plant of that variety may turn—by division and sub-division—into billions and billions of potatoes—all actually parts of that first plant. It would be interesting to know how many billion tons that first King Edward plant has developed into during its life!

It was thought once that this endless preservation of one individual must lead to vitiation or degeneracy and that every potato variety would, in the end, die out. This does not seem to be happening *provided* all 'seed', meaning not seed but *sets*, is grown in a cold enough country to prevent its attack by certain aphid-borne diseases. If you multiply potatoes year after year in your garden in Surrey you will find that after a very few years you will be growing fewer and fewer potatoes. Certain virus diseases will enter the plants via aphid attack and build up from year to year until you will be growing nothing but grossly diseased potatoes. That is why we nearly all buy 'seed potatoes' from such cold and wet places as the west of Scotland, Northern Ireland, or from farms over eight hundred feet above sea-level in Wales or England. Potatoes are now grown in India and there the 'seed' is grown at such places as Himachal Pradesh, in the hill country.

Potatoes are not frost-hardy, and if the plants are above the ground in a frost it will frizzle them. Thus early potatoes are grown in places near the coast like Cornwall, South Pembrokeshire, or the Channel Islands. Main crop potatoes are a different thing altogether —they produce much heavier yields than 'earlies' do, are left in the ground into late Autumn for there is no advantage in lifting them early, and can be stored either in *clamps*, which are long heaps covered with straw and then earth or, more and more nowadays, in buildings—sometimes even with CO_2 to prevent them going bad. If they can be kept chilled in the spring this stops them from sprouting, which makes them useless, or there are certain chemicals with which they are treated which have the same effect. What effect these chemicals have on *us* we are not told—maybe it is better to grow your own potatoes.

Yields of potatoes are very high: from eight to ten tons an acre is easily achieved with farmyard manure alone and fifteen tons is not uncommon nowadays. The crop likes very heavy manuring—twenty tons of farmyard manure is ideal. Thus the heart of the land is improved by a potato crop and also by its freedom from weeds, for potatoes need plenty of inter-row cultivation before they get big enough to become a 'smothering crop'—when they suppress weeds by cutting the light off from them with their foliage.

One of the most famous, or infamous, diseases in the world is *Blight* in potatoes, for it was this disease that reduced the population of Ireland from eight million to five million in the 1840s. As the absentee landlords of Ireland were in the habit of taking nearly the whole of the corn crops of their tenants straightaway as rent the Irish turned to the potato for their own food—for this could be stored by being left in the ground where the agents of the landlords could not get their hands on it. Potatoes are a crop that derives from the high Andes, where presumably blight is not a major problem. This microscopic fungus must have developed fairly secretly in European conditions until, in the forties of the last century, it struck with extraordinary virulence, wiping out practically the whole crop in Ireland in 1845 and 1846. People died in millions, and tens of thousands made the doleful journey down to the nearest port to be shipped off to America as destitute emigrants. It is noteworthy that during the whole course of the potato famine in Ireland the landlords continued to ship wheat and barley grown on that island to England. There is no doubt that potato blight was the prime cause of the present unrest in Northern Ireland. The I.R.A. could not exist without massive financial support from the Irish in America, and the descendants of the emigrants of the 1840s can never forget the circumstances which sent them there. It has been seriously suggested too that the collapse of the German armies in the First World War was due to the potato blight as much as the efforts of the Allied armies.

It was noticed that potatoes grown downwind from the great copper smelters at Swansea were immune from blight. This led to experiments with sprays made from copper, which were found to be more or less effective, but then the French, in their vineyards fighting another sort of fungal infection, invented Bordeaux Mixture and Burgundy Mixture, both compounds containing copper sulphate ('blue stone') and potatoes adequately sprayed with these will not get blight.

Nowadays highly sophisticated machinery is used for planting and havesting potatoes. Some of the harvesters are almost incredibly complicated, for they attempt to do what one might think impossible for a machine: tell the difference between a potato and a clod of earth the same size and the same density. Most machines, however, have men or women sitting in a row inspecting the potatoes (and clods) as they pass along a conveyor belt.

The aim of mechanized potato growers, though, is to cultivate their land so that they have no clods. Thus they do a minimum of mechanical cultivation once the spuds are planted but spray with herbicides which kill the weeds but don't too severely damage the potato plants, such as *linuron*. They also dip their sets in *menazon* or *dysiston* or plant *thimet* granules with the sets. These are systemic chemicals: that is they enter the very cell fluids of the plant, and grow up with it, and then defy aphids. *Metasystox* is extensively sprayed on the growing crop: this again is a systemic and penetrates to every cell of the plant. Of course traces of these chemicals are transferred to the potatoes of the new crop but nobody, so far, has died. A variety of sprays much stronger than the old Bordeaux and Burgundy Mixtures are now used against blight—among them *organo-mercury*, *organo-tin* and *copper-oxychloride*. Before harvest the *haulm* (tops) is commonly sprayed with *sulphuric acid*. This is to burn it up so that it won't be a nuisance to the complicated lifting machines. Finally the *ware* (meaning potatoes for sale for eating) is sprayed with *nonanol*, another chemical, to prevent it from sprouting in store. The writer sprays nothing but Bordeaux Mixture in bad blight years—and potatoes are coming out of my clamp now, May 12th, in perfect condition. We'll be lifting earlies next week anyway.

Turnips and *swedes*, which belong to the Brassica genus of the Cruciferous family (and are therefore closely related to cabbages) transformed English agriculture in the seventeenth and eighteenth centuries. This is because they are biennials. They store food the first year and then use it up by flowering, fruiting and seeding the next. The farmer can therefore use them in their first winter, when they have stored away nourishment which can feed the farmer's stock. There are many variations on turnips and swedes now— *Mangolds* for example (big red or yellow roots which may yield over twenty tons an acre) and which scientists are always telling farmers are nearly all water, to which the farmers reply 'But what water!' For, in spite of the analytical chemist, all water or no, we all know that mangolds will stimulate the milk yield amazingly. *Fodder Beet*, which is a close relative of sugar beet, is an excellent fodder for cattle, sheep and particularly pigs. It is much higher in dry matter and in protein than are mangolds but it doesn't have the colossal yield of mangolds. *Kohlrabi*, *Cabbages*, *Kale* (Marrow-stem, Curly, Hungry-gap are some varieties) *Fodder-radish*—are all other crops grown in the summer for feeding to stock in the winter.

The growing of all such fodder crops has declined greatly in recent years, because they are all labour-demanding crops. They need inter-row hoeing by tractor or horse, hand-hoeing at least twice, many of them need *singling*: the process of cutting out all the surplus plants in a row, when they are still tiny, with the hand-hoe. Therefore self-feed silage has taken the place of much 'root' growing on dairy and beef farms, and the practice of folding sheep on turnips (though having a slight revival just now) has almost died out altogether, being a labour-intensive method of keeping sheep.

Sugar Beet, however, holds its own, for it is heavily subsidized by the government. Complicated beet harvesters have almost displaced the man with a canvas apron and a 'beet-hook'—a short knife with a little hook at the end for hooking up the beet from the ground and slicing the top off. Monogerm seed and precision drilling and selective weed sprays have pretty well taken the place of the hand-hoe. Beet seeds come in little clusters, so that if you drop a cluster into the soil you will get several plants close together which must be singled with the hand-hoe. Monogerm seeds have been split into single seeds and, planted at the correct intervals, obviate the need for this. The beet are carried to the factories during the 'sugar campaign' season— from, say, September to some time after Christmas, and there turned into enormous mountains of the white crystals that are ruining the teeth and health of our generation.

Field Beans, *Tic Beans* or *Cattle Beans*, all the same, were, when I was a boy, an important 'winter corn' crop, albeit they are not in any way related to corn. But they took the place of, for example, winter wheat in the rotation. They were drilled in the autumn and harvested late next summer with the binder and stacked just as corn was stacked. In the winter they were threshed out in an ordinary threshing-drum and fed to stock. They are coming back into use slowly, as more and more corn-only farmers are finding that their land is deteriorating under them from the effects of white-straw monoculture. They are now harvested with the combine harvester. As protein for stock food from the tropics and from the sea becomes scarcer and more expensive it is likely that beans will become far more common in this country and the most urgent job of our plant breeders, research stations and all the rest of it should be to find good sources of protein that can be grown in this country. *Field Peas* are obvious candidates for this with beans. *Vining peas* are grown on a large scale in the eastern counties of England to supply such packing companies as Birdseye. The whole crop is grown under close super- vision and harvested very quickly when the peas are just ripe with huge vining machines. Frozen, or dried and resuscitated, such peas are the nearest that most city people nowadays get to fresh-picked garden peas. *Carrots* are grown in huge acreages on very light land, or the Fenland peats, for the market. *Celery* is grown almost exclu- sively in the Black Fens. There are large areas of the country given over to one or more market-garden crops. A few of such local specializations are *Brussels Sprouts* in Buckinghamshire, *Broccoli* in Cornwall and Pembrokeshire, *Spring Greens* and other brassica crops on the Isle of Thanet, various market garden crops in the fantastically rich Vale of Evesham and on the Plain of Ormskirk in Lancashire, tulip and daffodil bulbs around Spalding in the Lincolnshire Fens and glasshouse crops in the Lea Valley near London or around Worthing on the south coast.

There is one crop which is growing in importance in Britain and that is maize. Some very early varieties of this have been known to ripen in Britain: that is ripen their seed to the degree that the latter can be dried, stored, ground, or planted so it will germinate. But by far the greater part of the maize grown in these islands is grown from seed grown in hotter countries and is for fodder, not grain. It is either cut green and fed immediately to dairy cows, in that gap in July and August when the grass is not growing so well as it did in May and June, or, far more often, cut and chopped up and made into silage. It gives a great deal of bulk and tonnage per acre. It is conceivable that varieties might be bred that will ripen grain reliably in this climate in which case it would become an important crop. In all countries where maize *can* be grown successfully as a corn crop—maize *is* grown. It takes its place with wheat and rice as one of the great staple foods of the world.

An interesting minor crop is the *hop*. There are just over twenty thousand acres of this grown, the bulk in Kent, a few acres in Sussex and Hampshire and Surrey, another block in Herefordshire and Worcestershire. The plant belongs to the nettle family, and is a climbing perennial. It puts out an extensive root system, going down twelve feet or more if it can, sends up bines which grow so fast that you can almost see them grow up to twenty-five feet, and dies down completely in the winter time. The cones, which may contain the seed, are picked and used to flavour beer. A yellow substance called *lupulin* which forms in the cones contains the resins and essential oil that give the hop its tang.

Beer came to England in the fifteenth century. Before that *ale* was drunk. Ale was malt liquor—beer was malt liquor flavoured with hops. Hops came from Flanders and at first laws were passed against them as they were considered dreadfully un-English, but by 1520 hops had become accepted (the English liked the bitter taste—and also the use of hops preserves the beer to some extent) and became a commercial crop.

There are several varieties—the most widely grown rejoicing in the name of *Fuggle*, which it got from a Farmer Fuggle of Kent who developed it in the eighteenth century. In Britain a few male hop plants are planted among the more numerous female ones, so that the flowers get fertilized. The reason for this is that in our uncertain climate the sooner the flowering period is got over the better, and the less chance there is of fungoid disease. On the Continent male plants are deliberately eliminated so that the cones are seedless. For brewing lager beers seedless hops are best, and so English lager-brewers have to import continental hops, and English hops are not acceptable on the continental market. With our entry into the E.E.C. it was decided that the English hop growers would have to come into line with the continental ones—the aim being to make everybody in the world, and every product, exactly alike. Hop growers are controlled completely by the Hop Marketing Board, which is the only buyer they are allowed to sell to, and nobody can grow hops for sale without a licence from the Board.

The stringing and wiring of a hop field (a 'garden' in Kent and a 'yard' in the West Midlands) is a science and an art. The pattern of wires and strings is very complicated. Some of the work is still often done by men on tall stilts. Picking used to be done by jolly Cockneys in south-east England and by gypsies in the West Midlands and these people looked upon this seasonal job as an annual holiday with pay and everybody enjoyed the fun. Now it is done by machines back in the barn to which the bines are carried when they have been cut off. This saves labour (but also fun), and has the disadvantage that it is bad for the hop plants to have their bines cut off in full flower in the

rick in process of
being thatched
and
small circular rick

summer, before the goodness in them has had time to descend again to the roots in the natural dying-off process. As a result the plants don't last so long, nor are they so vigorous. The lack of vigour is being made up for, though, by the use of more artificial manures. The increase in hop diseases (of which there is a large number) is being combated with a whole battery of new chemicals, with names like demeton-S-methyl and oxydemeton-methyl and vamidothion.

After picking, by whatever means, the hops are carefully *kilned*, or dried in a kiln over, nowadays, electric heaters. Formerly it was coal. Sulphur is burned under the hops during this process to improve the colour and for other esoteric, almost mystical, reasons.

It is said that if you sleep on a pillow stuffed with hops it makes you sleep. I sleep anyway so I wouldn't know.

Chapter 8

The Domestic Animals of the Countryside

The *Horse*, in eclipse at the moment, may not stay in eclipse for long, so we may as well consider him in some detail in this book.

Horse-using people are unusual in this world: most of the world's draught animals are not horses—oxen, water buffalo, donkeys, mules, elephants, but not horses. Horses do not flourish in the tropics (they get a disease called horse-sickness from the bite of a mosquito—or another called nagana in tsetse-fly areas) and they require standards of care and treatment that do not obtain in the 'less-developed' countries of the world. Throughout south-east Asia, including much of China and India, the water buffalo is the principal draught animal. He is pretty versatile—you get him right up in the hill country of North India where there isn't, by and large, much water, or at least not enough for him to wallow in—but where he is at his prime is in tropical monsoon countries where he can spend his leisure nearly immersed in the warm water of a tank, river or lagoon. Most of the milk drunk in India (even in the drier areas) comes from water buffalo. In drier areas, however, the ox vies with the buffalo—and gradually replaces him as you get further from the tropics.

In Africa the ox is the draught animal in every area free from nagana. In nagana areas the draught animal tends to be the female of the human species. In the Western Cape of South Africa the mule is king—generally driven with great verve and brilliance (not to say abandon) by Cape Coloured men—people of mixed race as the mule is himself. In Namibia, Botswana, much of the Transvaal, Rhodesia (Zimbabwe), and low veld areas the donkey competes with the ox.

Spans of twenty donkeys, wearing breast-plates, often roughly made of such materials as old inner-tubes, but never collars, haul wagons and gangs of disc ploughs. In North Africa, the Near East, Pakistan, Persia and Afghanistan, donkeys compete with camels. The horse is a riding animal in those countries—never a draught one. In southern and eastern Europe mules, donkeys and oxen, slowly give way to the horse.

It is only in the temperate countries, and of those only the ones which have a fairly highly developed agriculture and civilization (the same thing) that you find the working farm horse in any numbers. And even in Europe the horse didn't take over from the ox until quite late in history.

The horse is much faster as a draught animal than the ox, and two horses can pull as much as four oxen—and faster. The horse requires better feeding, stabling, and better care generally. An ox will do quite a lot of work on grass alone: a horse must have corn (in Britain nearly always oats) to do many hours of work in a day. A horse on grass alone gets soft and out of condition. The ox has the advantage that throughout his working life 'he is growing into meat'. The practice in South Africa is to break cattle to the yoke when they are 'tollies' (eighteen-month old oxen), work them until they are three and thus fully grown, then let them fatten on grass for a few months and sell them to the butcher. On the Continent of Europe the same attitude is, alas, taken to horses. The people of these islands have an unshakeable objection to eating horses (I too abhor the idea!) but old or redundant horses are in fact eaten for they are either killed here and sent to the Continent or else exported on the hoof. This is the equivalent of the massive trade in smuggling surplus cattle across the border from India into Pakistan. The Indians will not eat cattle: the Muslims in Pakistan will.

The classic breeds of farm horses in Britain, all derived from the old war horse that had to carry the heavily armoured knights, are: the *Shire*, very heavy and large, up to seventeen hands (a hand is four inches and the measurement is from the ground to the withers), three-quarters of a ton in weight and a ton in the case of some stallions, much *feathered* as to the legs (long hair hanging down from the fetlock), slow-moving but enormously strong: the very archetype of the heavy working horse. The *Clydesdale* is as tall as a Shire but slightly lighter, longer in the leg and with a slightly smaller body, less feather, faster moving. The *Suffolk Punch*, also called just *Suffolk* or just *Punch*, is a stockier horse than either a Shire or a Clydesdale, with much shorter legs, though pretty heavy—a big stallion will also weigh a ton—and with the most *courage*, in my opinion anyway, of any horse in the world. A Suffolk will never give up trying to move a

Shire   Suffolk Punch

load. A French horse, the *Percheron*, came to this country in 1916 and proved immediately popular. It is fast-moving, willing and docile. Then there are endless compounds of all these: half-bred and quarter-bred horses of every size and description: *Irish Draughts*, *Half-Legs*, and of course the lighter types of cobs and ponies such as the *Welsh Cob* and the *Welsh Mountain*, *Dales*, *Fell*, *Exmoor*, *Dartmoor*, *Shetland* are all ponies. The demand for ponies for children to ride on has made the breeding of these a major industry, and now there is a demand for a larger, cob-type animal for the growing sport of 'trekking', which consists of people riding out in larger or smaller parties, under the guidance generally of a professional, and traversing large areas of countryside. Most of the mountain and moorland areas in Britain produce ponies or cobs as a crop: the mares running wild on the open range, with a stallion or two running with them, and being rounded up once a year (generally by a number of owners because very often this sort of country is common grazing) for the yearlings to be roped, thrown and castrated and branded if they are colts or just caught if they are fillies and are required for sale, loaded into horse boxes and taken to the lower land to be broken for the saddle. The word *broken* as applied to horses means simply *trained*— the last thing you want to do is to *break* a horse's spirit—training should be a matter of establishing confidence in the horse so that he or she trusts you and will do what you want.

But farm working horses, so almost completely eclipsed by the tractor, are making a slow come-back. As diesel oil gets dearer in relation to labour costs it becomes more and more possible to imagine the day when horses will come back. A man can plough an acre a day with a pair of good horses on medium land, from five to eight acres with a light tractor and maybe fifteen acres with a heavy one. Thus a heavy tractor is fifteen times as cost-effective in regard to labour as a pair of horses. But a heavy tractor costs five thousand pounds perhaps, the cost is continually going up, depreciation is heavy, oil is getting more and more expensive and who knows indeed if it will always be available? And no tractor yet has been known to have a foal. As long as we try to farm with practically no manpower the tractor will be a necessity. If ever *people* in numbers come back to the land, either because they want to or because they have got to because of the break-down of industrial society, then the horse will come into its own again.

A heavy working horse will need about twenty pounds or their equivalent of oats a day, and perhaps the same quantity of hay, when he is in full work only—that is doing the equivalent of his acre a day, but we may safely halve the oats figure for a working horse all the year round: there will be times when he is out on grass in which case he only needs perhaps ten pounds of oats for a full day's work or half that for half a day. So we may put it at a ton of oats for two hundred days of pretty hard work or maybe for a year of more normal work. Thus an acre of land will grow enough oats to feed a working horse for a year—an acre and a half perhaps if he works very hard. Add to this an acre of hay and a small share of the grazing of the farm during the summer time and you have about the right allowance. If you allow three acres of land to provide all the food for a heavy working horse you will not be far out. Considering that the horse requires practically nothing from outside the farm, and certainly nothing from outside the country, this is not bad. Also one must not forget the very valuable manure into which the horse turns most of the food he eats. But it is human labour which horse-work is prodigal of, and highly skilled and intelligent human labour at that.

The horseman's day on a conventional farm starts early: at half-past five or six. If the horses have been out on grass during the night he must go and catch them and bring them into the stable—in the winter they will be in the stable anyway—he must water them and *bait* them (give them a feed) and while they are feeding go and have his own breakfast. Horses must be given plenty of time to feed. He must then go and groom them, harness them up, take them out to the field and hitch them up. He may then work them for four hours, have two hours' break, and work for another four hours, leaving the field at perhaps four in the afternoon, (a 'two-yoke day') or he may work them through to say three o'clock, with only a couple of half-hour breaks (a 'one-yoke day') and without returning to the stable. When finally he does return he must bait them again, groom them well, clean his harness, and see that his horses are happy before he finally goes off to see to his own creature comforts.

A few farms have never given up horse-work. Farm horses are at present making a very slow come-back. But it is notable that if you prolong the present curves that depict cost-per-acre in the case of horse ploughing and of tractor ploughing, you find that although now tractor ploughing is by far the cheaper, the curves are tending to come together. My prediction is that by 1985 they will have crossed.

Cattle are kept for two purposes in Britain: to give milk and to provide beef. Formerly all our cattle were 'dual-purpose'—they did both. In the eighteenth century breeders got to work and gradually one-purpose breeds were developed, such as we have now.

British cattle husbandry is at present almost completely domin-ated by the *Friesian*: an import from the Netherlands. These are large, bony, black and white cattle that give a great deal of not very rich milk. One is always being assured by Friesian owners that efforts are being made by breeders to improve the butter-fat content of Friesian milk. I remember being assured about this in 1935. True, the butter-fat has gone up a little but it is still far below that of any other breed. But the differential in price that the Milk Marketing Board pays for higher butter-fat milk is so slight that there is no financial incentive to go in for higher butter-fat cows. Quantity is what pays, and quantity is what the Friesian gives in full measure.

Another reason for the overwhelming dominance of the black and white cow is that it has been found, in the last twenty years, that Friesian bull calves, and heifer calves surplus to replacement requirements, are very suitable for the kind of lean, quick-maturing beef beloved of the modern butcher. In eighteen months from birth a Friesian steer, housed and fed on an intensive diet, will be saleable as beef. It may be complained by people who remember what mature beef tasted like that this 'instant beef' isn't a patch on the old three-year-old beef from the beef breeds, and this is undoubtedly true; but owing to the rationing of the Second World War the British people more or less forgot what mature beef tasted like. Friesian cows crossed with Hereford bulls, or bulls of other beef breeds, also produce a fast-maturing lean beef animal, so most Friesian cows are mated with Hereford bulls to produce that animal with a black body and a white head that always fetches a good price in the auction ring. So Friesians score, both for milk quantity and for quick beef, and dominate our cattle herds.

Forty years ago the *Shorthorn* was still king. There were two strains: the Beef Shorthorn and the Dairy Shorthorn. The breed was developed in the Teeswater district, around Darlington, in the eighteenth century, probably with a mixture of the Celtic black blood, the red Anglo-Saxon cattle, and a strong injection of parti-coloured Dutch cattle blood. It was written of them, in 1743, that they had 'wide bags, short horns, and large bodies, which render 'em (whether black or red) the most profitable beasts for the dairy-man, grazier, and butcher.' The great classical breeders of the nineteenth and early twentieth centuries—Thomas Bates of Kirk-levington, Charles and Robert Colling of Ketton and Barmton near Darlington, the Booths of Killerby, Amos Cruikshank of Sittyton, Aberdeenshire, the Garnes of Aldsworth in the Cotswolds—devoted their lives to building up a magnificent breed of cattle. Bulls and cows were sold all over the world to grade up 'native' breeds to a higher standard of beef and milk production. Probably more than any other livestock the Shorthorn made British stock breeders famous throughout the world. The Shorthorn has, however, been almost knocked out in Britain now by the all-conquering Friesian, the *Ayrshire* (a white cow with red markings on her which vies with the Friesian as a bulk milk-producer but which is far less suitable for beef), and the more specifically beef breeds, used mostly

Friesian

Ayrshire

Jersey

for crossing with the Friesian, such as the *Hereford, Aberdeen Angus, Sussex, Devon, Galloway*, and new beef breeds imported from France such as the *Charollais* and *Simenthal*.

The Hereford has also spread over the world—in both North and South America more cattle have Hereford blood than that of any other breed. It is a fine-looking beast with a rich red body and invariably a white head, and this white head is impressed on any other breed it crosses with. The *South Devon* is a dual-purpose breed which is just about holding its own, the *Red Poll* another which is not holding its own. The *Welsh Black*, a mountain breed from the ancient Celtic strain, is very much holding its own, for it is proving a good beef breed particularly in the mountains of Wales.

The Channel Island breeds, *Jersey* and *Guernsey* are much used for house cows, and there are also herds of them kept by farmers who are not quite so money-orientated as some others. They give by far the richest milk of any, there is a premium price paid for it by the Milk Marketing Board but not enough differential to make them really competitive with the Friesian. The Jersey, in particular, is the most docile of animals, and a Jersey house cow is apt to become a family pet and it is difficult to keep her out of the drawing-room. The bull calves of both Channel Island breeds are of no account for beef, having yellowish fat which doesn't look good on the butcher's slab, therefore most bull calves are killed for veal. The *West Highland*,

Welsh Black Cattle

made famous by Landseer and other sentimental Victorian artists, is a shaggy animal with wide-swept horns that looks rather like a yak. It is very slow maturing but makes very good beef.

As for the methods by which cattle are kept, these are many and various.

In hill areas, and other areas of marginal fertility, 'single-suckling' herds are kept: maybe of Herefords or other beef cattle and, in Wales and more and more, Welsh Blacks. The cows are simply allowed to run on more or less free range, with a bull put in with them at the appropriate time; they have calves in due course, and suckle them—each cow her own calf and no more. Generally the calves are born in the spring, they grow marvellously all summer for their mums are on summer grass, and are sold at special 'suckled-calf sales' in the autumn. They are generally bought by fatteners who put them indoors the first winter and feed them well on hay, barley and other concentrates, probably turn them out to grass the next spring, and perhaps sell them fat in the autumn. If they don't 'grade' by autumn—that is pass as acceptable butchers' animals— then they may have to be expensively housed and fed for part of another winter.

Then there is *multiple suckling*. A man may keep a herd of cows, allow them to calve, then buy more calves in from the market (called 'mart' in the west and north) when they are a week old, and try to foist these on the cow that has just calved as her foster children. Some cows will take foster calves like this and you can simply turn them out and forget them. More often you have to bring the cow in twice a day and tie her up and watch her while her foster children suck. It is a very trying and laborious way of earning a living, and many of the calves that you buy at a week old die before they are much older of *scours*—an infection of the alimentary canal.

Farmers also buy week-old calves in the mart, or straight from their breeders, and rear them 'on the bucket' with milk-substitute, generally reinforced powdered milk. This again is risky and losses are high. But the fact is that the average milk producer just does not *want* his calves. He wants to be rid of them as soon as may be, for he is selling milk and so doesn't want to give it to calves. Some milk producers combine milk with beef production and rear their calves up on milk substitute and turn them into beef. Most get rid of them for what they can get.

Calves running out of doors with their mothers never seem to be ill. They can be born on top of a mountain in a blizzard in December (many are) and they survive perfectly well. But calves taken away from their mothers too early are heir to many diseases. If you turn them out on grass in the spring or summer they will very likely get *husk*, a disease caused by a worm in the lung (if they are with their mothers they get husk, but so mildly that nobody knows about it) and they will die. Thus they have to be housed for the first year of their lives as a rule, and this is expensive.

As for how beef cattle are kept during the latter part of their lives: some are fattened out on grass during the summer time on 'fattening pastures', which are very good and valuable pastures covering only a limited part of the country such as the Welland Valley, the Norfolk Broadland, the Severn Valley, Romney Marsh, or other very favoured alluvial soil areas. Most cattle are fattened indoors, either on self-feed silage as we discussed in our chapter on Buildings, on barley (the 'barley-beef' craze a decade ago made and broke a lot of farmers), or in the good old-fashioned way of keeping them on deep wheat straw and feeding them on a concentrate of perhaps wheat-meal, barley-meal, rolled oats—all stuff that can be grown on the farm—some hay, and chopped oat straw, together with mangolds or fodder beet or turnips or other succulents. This method is labour-intensive but produces the best beef and furthermore mountains of good *muck*, of farmyard manure, the basis of all sound agriculture. If depression in the cities ever forces people back on to the land this is what we will come back to.

As for where the fatteners get their *stores* from (a store is an adult steer or heifer which is not yet fattened)—well, most come from the upland areas where the grass is not good enough to fatten (or 'finish') them, and corn is not grown to fatten them indoors; many come from Ireland, Wales, Scotland, the Pennines, and other such upland areas. There was once a great trade in Welsh and Scottish 'runts' as they were called: Welsh Black or West Highland, which were driven down from the uplands along the drove tracks by a race of men called drovers who did this for a livelihood. It is interesting that these men, being entrusted with large sums of money by the owners of the cattle, eventually went into a form of banking, and I have heard that drovers were the originators of several of our banks in this country, including Lloyds. The 'runts' were bought by Midland and Norfolk fatteners and fattened on grass or in yards. It was the Cardiganshire drovers, incidentally, who established the milk-distribution trade in London, and this is still largely in the hands of their descendants.

As for dairy cows, for years the production of whole milk has been the only growth industry in British agriculture. The reason for this is that fresh whole milk cannot be economically imported. The governments of Britain are purely urban in constitution and sentiment, for only three per cent of Britons are connected with the land

and that is a negligible voting body, therefore the policy of successive governments, since the repeal of the Corn Laws, has been simple! Charge duty, or place a total ban, on all imported manufactured goods, but allow all agricultural and horticultural produce in duty-free. Milk has been about the one thing the foreigners couldn't send us economically and therefore there has been a fair price for it.

Most cows in this country are run out on grass in the summer time but kept indoors in the winter, and we have discussed the various methods of housing them in Chapter 4. Dairy cows are commonly fed a *maintenance ration* and a *production ration*. Good hay alone can be a maintenance ration—that is it maintains the animal in good health but without producing milk. The production ration may well be corn of some kind, and/or imported 'cake'. The latter is probably derived from tropically grown oil seed of one sort or another, there may be fish-meal in it, and other high protein substances.

Nearly all dairy cows in this country are milked by machine. A suction pump in a shed adjoining the cowshed provides vacuum to a pipeline that runs through the milking shed, suction cups are placed over the cow's teats (perhaps four cows are milked at a time) and the milker is kept busy watching to see if a cow is finished, and removing her cups and placing them on another cow. In small herds the milk goes straight into a stainless steel bucket, which is emptied by hand into a churn at intervals. In larger herds it goes by pipeline into a bulk tank, often going through sophisticated weighing and recording gear first. In all cases milk is rapidly cooled, either by a cold water heat-exchanger or by refrigeration. Much milk is still put on the road every morning in milk churns to be picked up by the Milk Marketing Board lorries, but nowadays more and more is going into bulk tanks and being taken away by tanker.

Milking a large herd by machine is an exacting operation, and the milker has to be on his toes all the time. A farm worker who milks over a hundred cows twice a day (and many a man does) except for his statutory annual holiday, is a man under great strain, and many a farmer who cannot afford to employ a man does this for three hundred and sixty-five days a year and three hundred and sixty-six in Leap Years. Christmas Day is milking day just as any other: to miss a day would be to have your cows go dry, and cause mastitis and various other complaints. Mastitis, a disease of the udder in cows as in women, is universal among large herds milked by machine. It just cannot be eradicated. When it is spotted (often days or weeks after it has begun its course in a cow and after gallons of infected milk have gone into the churns or bulk tanks) penicillin is injected into the affected quarters. The milk of such penicillin-affected cows is not supposed to be sold for a period but this rule is more honoured by some farmers in the breach than the observance and there is always a proportion of penicillin in commercial milk. In *theory* a sample of the milk from each cow should be hand-milked before the cups are put on to examine for mastitis but go in and watch the milking of the next big milking herd you come to and see if this actually happens. With hand-milked cows it is immediately obvious if a cow starts mastitis, but in any case the disease is much less likely to spread in hand-milked cows. Small herds anyway are much less prone to it than big ones.

Sheep, like cows, are very versatile animals. In the Middle Ages they were kept primarily for wool, then the biggest export industry of England, but now—in Britain at least—wool is a minor consideration. Mutton, too, is nearly a thing of the past—that is the meat of sheep over a year old. Fat lamb is what sheep are kept for now, and the fuller, much more subtle flavour of mature mutton is something that most people in Britain have never experienced.

Welsh ram

Cheviot

Swaledale

The many breeds of British sheep may be classified into three groups: Mountain, Moorland and Hill, and Lowland.

Among Mountain breeds we would include: Welsh Mountain, Scotch Blackface, Swaledale, Herdwick (from the Lake District), Rough Fell, Lonk, Derbyshire Gritstone (these three are Pennine breeds), Cheviot, Exmoor Horn, Shetland. Of Moorland and Hill (intermediate between Mountain and Lowland) we have the Kerry Hill, Clun Forest and Radnor Forest: all from a very small area on the Wales-England border. Of the Lowland Breeds there are the *Short Wools*: Dorset Horn, Wiltshire Horned, Ryeland, Devon Closewool, and the Down Breeds: Southdown, Shropshire, Suffolk,

Dorset Down, Hampshire Down, Oxford Down. Then there are the Lowland *Long Wools*: Leicester, Border Leicester, Lincoln Longwool, Wensleydale, Cotswold, Kent or Romney Marsh, Devon Longwool, South Devon, Improved Dartmoor.

As if this plethora of sheep breeds were not enough (no other country—or even *continent*—has anything like this number of sheep breeds) there are many half-breeds which are so popular as almost to constitute distinct types. Thus the Border Leicester-Cheviot (the result of a Border Leicester ram on a Cheviot ewe) once looked like ousting all the breeds of the lowlands as the Friesian looks like ousting all breeds of dairy cows. It is not so prevalent now, however. The Suffolk-Welsh Mountain cross is very popular in the lower parts of Wales.

Now there are many quite different ways of keeping sheep.

On the high mountains, as one might expect, only the high-mountain breeds of sheep can be kept successfully. These have to be hardy enough to survive the gales and blizzards of mountain winters —the terrible 'white storms' that kill seasoned mountaineers—and rear their lambs often in conditions of snow and intense frost. They have to be *hefted*—that is born on and accustomed to their particular grazing range, for often the mountain grazing is not fenced. To turn out strange sheep on such ranges would be merely to lose them. When you buy a sheep farm you have to buy the sheep too: without complete fencing you cannot introduce new sheep. In order to ensure that first-year ewes (a ewe is a female sheep) grow adequately during their first winter, the custom is to send them down to the low country where they are 'put out on tack'. This means that the lowland farmer keeps them on his land for the winter, charging so much a head for doing so: currently five pounds per head for the winter. This is a heavy charge on the mountain farm and instead some mountain men are going over to buying hay and keeping their young ewes for the first winter on this, in a confined paddock near the house. After a ewe on the mountains has had three lambs she is unlikely to do well if kept there, for her teeth are beginning to wear away owing to having to chew the rough heather and mountain grasses. Therefore the ewes that have had three crops of lambs are sold to farmers down in the hills or lowlands. They will then give a further two or three crops of lambs before they are sold off as 'crones' for slaughter, and probably pet food.

So the mountain farmer almost invariably breeds his own replacement stock. The lowland farmer may keep a 'flying flock': that is he buys older ewes from the mountains, lambs them once, twice or three times, then sells them off.

Sheep in the lowlands suffered a great decline in this century, but are slowly coming back again. I even saw several flocks in Holland this year: where few sheep have been seen for centuries! Sheep do much good on grassland grazed by cattle during the summer: the sheep put on in the winter will eat the surplus grass left by the cattle, clean the pasture up, manure it and improve it with the treading of their hoofs, and ingest the parasitic worms which the cattle have left there so as to break the chain of infection for the cattle. Mixed stocking is always ecologically sounder than one-species stocking. And with a much better price for fat lamb sheep are coming back.

A way of keeping sheep that was widespread a hundred years ago and then almost died out, but which is slowly creeping back again, is folding on arable land.

The downland breeds of sheep were bred for this and nothing else. Such sheep were, and still occasionally are, kept exclusively on arable land with never a blade of grass to eat. Most, however, spend the summer on grass (mostly temporary leys), and the winter on arable land. Special crops are grown for them: swedes, turnips, a new crop called Hardy Greens that has been developed from the turnip, rape and kale. The sheep are confined in hurdles, or wire netting, and moved on to a new stretch of the crop each day. When they are moved on, a back-fence is established so they cannot move back on to land on which they have already been. Thus they never graze 'foul ground': land on which they have already excreted worm eggs, and they remain very healthy. The good they do to the land by their treading and manuring is great. It is, though, a labour-intensive way of keeping sheep. Incidentally the chalk downs and thin-soiled limestone hills such as the Cotswolds used to be farmed extensively with folded sheep. When I wrote in an earlier chapter that it is wrong to plough up the chalk downs for corn monoculture, I certainly did not mean that it was wrong to plough up the grassland there from time to time to grow crops for folding sheep, and then to take a corn crop or two and put it down to grass again. This was the regime practised extensively on the Wiltshire and Hampshire downs, the Cotswolds, and in many other places of dry, thin, upland soil. The light lands of Norfolk fell into this class: the 'golden hoof' of the sheep made farming possible in the Norfolk and Suffolk Brecklands for centuries. In the nineteenth century, agricultural depression and the pheasant craze combined to knock folded sheep out of the Brecklands, to replace them by pheasant-rearing for 'sport', and the

Brecklands returned to wilderness. The Forestry Commission moved in and took the whole of this area and planted it with conifers so the farmer is ousted for good there.

The language of sheep men varies from district to district and can be a puzzle to the uninitiated. Female lambs can be *ewe lambs*, *gimmer lambs* or *chilver lambs* depending upon where you are. Ram lambs after castration are *wether lambs*; when they cease to be lambs they are *hogs*, *hoggets* or *tegs*. Sheep that have had their first shearing —generally in the second summer of their lives because most breeds of sheep are not shorn the first summer—are *shearlings*, and, in the case of females, *gimmers* in the north and *theaves* in certain parts of the south. Sheep, like horses, can be aged by their teeth, and thus you hear sheep men talking about 'two-tooth', 'three-tooth' etc.— right up to 'full-mouth'.

The shepherd's or sheep-farmer's life varies according to what system of sheep husbandry he practises. The mountain farmer depends entirely on his dogs: he would have no chance whatever of farming sheep on the mountains without them. The dog can move over the mountains at great speed, and the sheep immediately react to him. They gather together and move in the direction in which the dog, or generally dogs, wish them to go. The master can control his dog as long as the latter can hear his shrill whistles—but often the dog works far out of sight and hearing of his master—he knows what is required of him and does it. It would be physically impossible for a farmer ever to round up sheep on a vast stretch of mountain without dogs.

Sheep on the mountains and hills keep much fitter than those further down. They never get foot-rot, a serious disease of sheep on soft lush pasture, and they never get 'struck' by fly. Fly-strike is a killing disease of sheep in the valleys—anywhere below five or six hundred feet in fact. A brilliantly coloured green fly lays eggs on the dirty part of a sheep—generally the soiled wool around the tail. The maggots hatch out and eat right into the sheep—they will, in time, eat the sheep alive. Valley farmers have to guard against this either by dipping the sheep (generally after shearing) in a substance which is poisonous to the maggot, or by spraying them, or else by constant vigilance—catching and treating with disinfectant any sheep that looks uneasy, or stands about twitching its tail in a manner that sheep farmers know all too well.

The mountain sheep farmer makes frequent excursions into his range to look at his sheep, move them perhaps on to what he thinks is better pasture, or, in some cases, he may leave them alone and never interfere with them until he has to muster them for some purpose. The purposes are: shearing, in June or July; drafting out

the first-year ewes to go down to the low country to spend their first winter;—maybe in October—drafting out fat lambs or lambs which he wishes to sell to the lowlands as stores; drafting out old ewes to be sold to the low country (any ewe that has had three lamb crops or over); in the winter trying to keep the sheep on the lower slopes and more sheltered places for fear of deep snow, and when the latter comes and even the hardiest of mountaineers keep to their huts, fighting his way through the snow, with his best dog, for the latter to nose out the whereabouts of buried sheep so that his master can dig them out of the snow with a spade. A sheep can, if not so discovered, survive for ten days or so completely buried in snow— in a cavity melted by the heat of her body and with a blow-hole her warm breath has made for air. In such circumstances sheep sometimes eat the wool off their own bodies. When one considers that sheep thrive in some of the hottest deserts of the world the versatility of this species, given to it by the selective breeding of man, can be seen to be amazing.

In the spring the mountain farmer must bring his ewes down to lower ground, in Wales perhaps to what he calls *y ffridd*—slightly improved and fenced lower slopes of the mountain. He must then keep a constant eye on them while they are lambing (the dog is left very much in the background then, both so as not to disturb them and also because a ewe with a lamb will take no notice of a dog and the dog is frightened of her). He will not give the lambing ewes the same intensive care that the lowland farmer will—there simply isn't time. In any case many of the ewes may well be lambing high up in the mountains, for not all of them get brought down. After lambing there may be castrating and docking to do, although many mountain farmers do neither: the ram lambs 'grade' (pass the inspection of the government 'officer' that they are fit to receive a government subsidy) before they develop very ram-like qualities and become unfit for killing for 'fat lamb'. Docking is the cutting off of the tail of young lambs and is supposed to help prevent 'fly-strike'. Both docking and castrating are nowadays done with the aid of tight rubber rings which cut off the circulation. Old-fashioned shepherds still castrate by cutting off the end of the scrotum and drawing out the 'stones' (testicles) with their teeth.

The work of the shepherd of the lowlands or downlands, who herds sheep on 'roots' or any arable land crop, is hard indeed. Every morning he must let the sheep run forward into another block of land, then carry the back hurdles forward and set them up, with stakes, to enclose another block of land for tomorrow. The hurdles are very heavy, and so are the stakes. He uses a heavy iron tool called in some parts a *sheep-bar*, in others (such as Suffolk) a *fold-pritch*, to drive holes for his stakes and then to knock the stakes in with. The use of the 'beetle' or 'bittle' (a huge wooden mallet) for this job is the sign of the amateur. If the shepherd uses wire netting instead of hurdles he has to roll up and carry forward the heavy rolls of netting. Further, if he is folding off turnips, he has to chop the turnips out of the ground with a mattock, for the sheep otherwise can only eat the top half. Generally, too, he has to feed the sheep with hay, and also possibly some corn.

Gloucestershire shepherd's song

We shepherds are the best of men
That e'r trod English ground.
When we come to an ale-house
We value not a crown!
We spend our money freely
We pay before we go
      There's no ale
      On the Wolds
      Where the stormy winds do blow!

That man would be a shepherd
Must have a valiant heart,
He must not be faint-hearted
But boldly play his part!
He must not be faint-hearted
Be it rain or frost or snow
      There's no ale
      On the Wolds
      Where the stormy winds do blow!

When I kept sheep on Blockley Hill
It made my heart to ache
To see the yows hang out their tongues
And hear the lambs to blate
But I plucked up my courage
And o'er the hills did go
      Pennéd them
      In the folds
      While the stormy winds did blow!

As soon as I had enfolded them
I turned my back in haste
And went unto an ale-house
Good liquor for to taste,
For drinks and jovial company
They are my heart's delight

While my sheep
Lie asleep
All the forepart of the night!

Pigs are quite a different animal to any other the farmer deals with. For one thing they are omnivorous, and only partially grazing animals. Pigs will eat grass, particularly good growing grass, but they cannot live on it. In medieval times the few sows and even fewer boars needed for breeding were just kept alive during the spring and summer, then they—and their offspring—were turned out into the woods during autumn to thrive and fatten on acorns and beech-mast and other seeds of the trees. The pigs to be killed were all killed before Christmas and either eaten or salted—and the breeding stock just kept alive until acorn-time again.

A sow has two litters a year under normal circumstances, and a litter varies from six or seven to as many as eighteen or twenty. About ten or twelve is most usual, and we would all rather a sow had eight good ones and did them well than sixteen runts and some of them died. Nowadays agribusinessmen are avid to make sows have more than two litters a year and so they wean the piglets very early— some almost immediately—and put them on milk-substitutes. The sow will then 'take the boar' in a few days. We old-fashioned farmers prefer to leave the piglets on for at least eight weeks (some people leave them for as much as twelve weeks). The piglets are then weaned and either sold to a fattener who fattens them in a house, or else they are fattened on the farm. Sows are much healthier if they are allowed to run out of doors. Pigs being fattened do so more quickly, and on less food, if warmly housed. If you run pigs out of doors, though, you must either give them a very big run or you must change their run occasionally—otherwise there will be a build-up of parasitic worms. This has led farmers with huge herds to house their sows too. This leads to various complications: disease build-up in the houses (combated by high-pressure steam hoses between farrowings), breaking of the 'chain of instinct' of the sow causing her to lie on or even eat her piglets, and other evils. Thus such farmers have been forced to confine breeding sows in crates, where they cannot get up or turn round, and the piglets are lured away from the mother by

144

infra-red lamps and only go back to the mother to suckle. Thus one artificiality leads to another artificiality. The piglets, kept on concrete, cannot eat earth and they get anaemia and have to be injected with iron (outdoor piglets *never* get anaemia) and we are led, in the end, to the obscenity of the sows being killed by a vet as soon as they start farrowing and the piglets being cut living from the dying womb, to be reared under aseptic conditions as 'disease-free pigs' to form a 'minimal-disease herd'. This is a system being practised more and more by agribusinessmen in this country, in the secrecy of the Belsen houses. The majority of real farmers, I am glad to say, abhor such practices.

But the *greed* of the urban-minded factory-farmer is what causes him to resort to such measures. When every farmer kept a few sows and a boar the animals were very profitable, great eaters-up of waste such as whey or skimmed milk or tail corn or 'chat' spuds (very small potatoes), and could be run out of doors and kept very healthy. It is only when a businessman wants to keep pigs in hundreds—or even thousands—and really make big money out of pigs and pigs alone— that the problems build up and obscene solutions have to be applied. The pig is an intelligent animal, and it is delightful to see pigs running and gambolling about in the open air, and rooting deep down into the earth as nature intended them to do. To confine the pig in a small house for life, on concrete where he can never root, is cruelty, and to force sows to farrow in crates, and deny them the proper use of their instincts—which normally cause them to go through an elaborate nest-making procedure, carrying straw in their mouths from here to there and carefully making a nest—is an unworthy thing to do. I kept sows for eight years in Suffolk, always out of doors but with small movable huts for them to farrow in, gave them plenty of straw for nest-making, they gave me quite monotonously twelve good piglets twice a year each, and in all that time only two piglets were killed by being lain on and none were eaten. When they farrowed I never went near them, and that is the best way. I could not have kept a hundred sows like this, though.

It must be stressed, however, that there are two distinct operations in the farming of pigs. One is breeding, and the other is fattening. Generally the two jobs are done by different people, although not always. The breeder rears the piglets to what are called *weaners* —piglets from about eight to twelve weeks old. They are then sold, either privately, in the market, or through a 'weaner group'—a kind of co-operative—to the fattener. He puts them indoors and feeds them very carefully measured quantities of highly concentrated food —until they are ready for slaughter. He keeps them indoors because they 'convert their food' better if kept warm. In many cases nowadays, pigs are kept by agribusinessmen in total darkness—relieved only when the light goes on three times a day for feeding. This stops fighting. Pigs *can* be fattened in pleasant, airy, straw-bedded pens though, and allowed to run out into the sun, and although they may not 'convert their food' with quite such a high degree of efficiency, they will be much happier, and healthier too. Further, they will be producing tons of very valuable manure to put on the land. But this is a labour-intensive way of keeping pigs, and can only be done if there is plenty of manpower.

When pigs fitted well into the economy of the mixed farm was when the farmer, or his wife, made butter or cheese or both. Separated milk from the butter-making, and whey from the cheese-making, were most excellent pig foods, and pigs would fatten readily on a diet of whey or separated milk with some barley meal and maybe bran or other wheat offals. There was a benign circle here—the cows helped feed the pigs, the pigs produced manure to help grow the cows' fodder, and the farmer reaped the benefit in the form of good butter and cheese and also bacon and ham.

Butter- and cheese-making have been killed almost completely in England on a farm scale by government policy. Cheese and butter imports have been allowed in very freely from other countries which have a longer grazing season than ours and in which therefore these products can be made very cheaply, and from countries which have heavily subsidized their exports, and also the Milk Marketing Board has used butter- and cheese-making as a method of disposing of surplus milk during the summer gluts. Therefore this benign circle— grass—cows—pigs—land—grass no longer works to turn out fine farm produce and improve our land.

As for the final form in which pigs go to market: they can be fattened as *porkers, cutters, baconers* or *heavy hogs.* Porkers are quite small pigs, sold straight to the butcher who cuts them up and sells them as fresh pork. Cutters are somewhat bigger and cater perhaps for more robust tastes in the north of England and other places. Baconers all go to the handful of large bacon factories in the country and are cured by a process of being steeped in brine in tanks, and sometimes thereafter smoked, into bacon and ham. Heavy hogs are a fairly new development. In days of old the Englishman liked his bacon enormously fat. His descendants, being a sedentary people, cannot eat much fat bacon and therefore the modern baconer is a lean animal. The idea of the heavy hog is that a pig is fattened to enormous proportions and the fat is then trimmed off the lean. The lean goes for pork pies, sausages, tinned ham and other industrial uses, while the fat goes for lard or manufacturing. The huge sausage and pie factories absorb the heavy-hog production.

As for breeds of pig—the British pig was modified and improved at the beginning of the nineteenth century by the introduction of *Sus vittatus*, the wild pig of eastern Asia. The European species is *Sus scrofa*: the wild boar of Europe. The Asian pig has a shorter and wider head than the European, and this has impressed itself on all our breeds, with the possible exception of the Tamworth, which still has the long pointed snout of the European wild boar or the domesticated pig of medieval times.

Perhaps the most widespread of our modern breeds up until thirty years ago was the *Large White*, developed by the mill-hands and miners of Yorkshire in their back gardens. In 1851 a weaver

Large White

Wessex Saddleback

of Keighley, Joseph Tulley, exhibited a vast pig at the Royal Show at Windsor and aroused great interest, and no doubt most Large Whites in existence now have some of the blood of this pig. The Large White has prick ears (that is its ears stand up) and is thus bad for keeping behind the electric fence. It can see too much and will charge through. It also has something of the long face of the Tamworth, or the European wild pig.

The *Middle White* is not found now in great numbers. It used to put on too much fat. The *Berkshire* suffered much the same fate for much the same reason. The *Large Black* may sometimes still be used for crossing—a Landrace boar on Large Black sows. The result of all such white/black cross is what is known as a 'blue' pig: white with bluish patches. Many outdoor pig keepers believe black pigs are hardier than white ones out of doors, but the modern butcher or bacon factory does not like a black pig. Thus this cross.

The *Wessex* and the *Essex* are the two 'saddleback' pigs. They are black with white marks over their backs above their white front legs. The Wessex was the forest pig of the New Forest: the Essex, some people say, of Epping Forest. They hold their own fairly well as pigs to be crossed to a white boar in open-air pig keeping.

The *Tamworth* was the cottage pig of the industrial workers of the Birmingham district. They are reddish in colour. They have practically died out, but the breed is being revived now for the value of its genetic stock. The *Gloucestershire Old Spots* is also enjoying a very modest come-back, due to the fact that the individual farmer here and there is becoming tired of too much uniformity. I can say from personal experience that it is a fine outdoor pig, has large litters, and crosses well with the white breeds. There are various minority breeds like the *Cumberland, Lincoln Curly Coat, Ulster*, all of which are white and have lop-ears, but except for the genetic pool these breeds are pretty negligible. The *Welsh*, a long, lean, white, lop-eared pig, has gained greatly in popularity recently and is becoming one of the foremost breeds. It has much Swedish Landrace blood in it.

And last we come to the *Swedish Landrace*, which is to pig-keeping in Britain what the Friesian is to milk production.

The Danes developed their native pig, called the Landrace, to a pig perfectly suited to modern conditions and the modern market. It has great length, great leanness and very good food conversion. The Danes will not let any live Landrace be exported and no one yet has had the initiative to smuggle some stock out of the country. The Swedes, however, managed to acquire some Danish Landrace blood

Welsh boar

before the ban on exports was applied, and have their own brand of Landrace, and this we have introduced into this country. It is a lean, white, long, lop-eared pig. It thrives better in indoor conditions than outdoors and its crosses are the commonest pigs in Britain today.

Poultry. Nowadays most eggs in this country are laid by hens which are kept in batteries. These hens are hatched from eggs laid by foundation stock normally kept in deep-litter houses (hens kept in batteries being infertile), hatched in incubators, reared in vast houses in brooders, and introduced into the wire battery cages when they are on point of lay—in other words just when they are going to start laying eggs. They are then kept in the batteries—two or three to a tiny cage—with food and water automatically supplied in front of the cage; their eggs, as they lay them on the wire, rolling down to be caught in a trough in front and then often taken out of the house by conveyor belt, their droppings falling through the wire and being taken away also by conveyor belt. I am afraid that battery hen 'farming' is one branch of agribusiness that I have had little personal experience of—I cannot stand the stench of a battery house, nor the manifest cruelty, nor the human degradation involved. I would not eat a battery egg if I could possibly avoid it.

Poultry for meat are generally kept in *deep-litter houses*. It was dis-covered that if chickens are crowded together on deep litter of any sort—it may be straw, wood shavings, sawdust, or any other organic waste, the litter ferments, giving off heat, reducing the smell of chicken manure, decaying the manure very quickly, remaining dry, and forming a satisfactory floor for chickens. The *broiler industry* is founded on this fact. Chickens are crowded into deep-litter houses, fed *ad lib*, kept in dim light so they do not cannibalize each other (although many still do) and then slaughtered. Their meat is as tasteless as one would expect it to be.

Chickens are still kept by some enlightened farmers on free range, that is they are allowed to run over grassland or in woodland, or on the stubble fields after harvest to pick up the spilt grain, or on freshly ploughed land where they do enormous good by eating wireworm and leather-jackets, and these hens keep healthy and lay well, find much of their food for themselves, do the land good by manuring it and scrapping on it, eat weed seeds, but do not lay quite as many eggs in a year as battery hens, who have nothing else to do but lay eggs. Such hens are best kept in movable houses, so they can be taken from field to field as circumstances require. This again is a labour-intensive way of farming, and also it cannot be done with very large numbers. As long as the townsman insists on having his food for far less than it costs to produce decently, and as long as manpower is short on the land, most eggs will have to come from the Belsen houses.

As for breeds of chicken, battery hens are carefully bred hybrids, designated by numbers, produced by enormous hatcheries which specialize in doing just this. They lay prodigiously for one laying season and then are scrapped, for by then they are grossly diseased anyway. They are never kept on for a second year and no battery hen lives longer than eleven months. I have had hens out of doors laying well after eight years! Broiler chickens are another kind of hybrid, bred and produced in the same sort of way.

As for the old breeds of fowl—still found in backyards and scratching round the barnyards of enlightened farmers—they are divided into three main groups, table breeds, laying breeds, and dual-purpose. It would be too much to describe them all here, beyond saying that the *Light Sussex* is a very common table breed, the *White Leghorn* a very fine layer, the *Rhode Island Red* perhaps the most successful hen in the world and dual-purpose. A monument has been erected to this breed on Rhode Island in America! Several of the old *game* breeds: *Old English Game, Indian Game*, etc., have been developed as very fine table breeds. Gypsies, and many farmers too, love to see *bantams* around. These are miniature chickens and can be of various breeds. The cockerels of these, and some of the game breeds, can be as gorgeous as peacocks: living jewels. Cock-fighting is no longer allowed, but is carried on in the Black Country, and extensively by Gypsies up and down the country. After all, when two families of Travelling People meet, the bantams or game-cocks have to be let out of the caravans and—if they fight—who can stop them? In any case their masters may be too busy placing bets.

Ducks are kept intensively, but out of doors, on light-land farms principally in the Brecklands of Norfolk. Hatched and reared artificially they are kept in huge mobs behind wire netting. They are not given access to water to swim on as they can survive without it.

Geese don't lend themselves to agribusiness methods and therefore are ignored by the agribusinessman. They are a grazing animal and can live on grass alone, and are kept in small numbers on many small farms. Only during the last three weeks of their lives (generally just before Christmas) are they fed with much corn to fatten them.

Turkeys do lend themselves to factory-farming, unfortunately, and are kept in huge houses and fattened for Christmas and other high days and holidays.

Chapter 9

The Wild Animals of the Countryside

The mammals that are truly indigenous to the British Isles would make a very short list, and the reason for this is twofold: the last Ice Age and the fact that we are an island.

The last four ice ages, the only ones we know much about, stretched from about a million and half years ago to about ten thousand years ago. These were interspersed with four interglacial periods during which the weather got quite warm: in fact possibly sub-tropical. As the glacial periods developed, and the ice advanced south, it was possible for the animals to retreat before it, for Britain was not an island. Conversely when the ice retreated it was possible for the animals to advance back. The time-scale, too, was such that species had time to evolve by natural selection so as to be able to cope with the extremes of climate that existed between the peaks of the glacials and the interglacials. Thus during the glacials there were such creatures as woolly rhinoceros, mammoth, reindeer, musk ox, arctic fox; during the interglacials more tropical creatures like hippopotami worked north again.

But after the last glacial (called the Weichsel Glaciation), which lasted about fifty thousand years until about 8000 B.C., Britain was severed from the mainland. Man was one of the mammals to get across after the ice had gone but before the land bridge was cut by the sea, and thereafter he continued to come because by Mesolithic times he had invented the boat and could cross the narrow Channel. But of other mammals only the ones which had got across before the Channel cut through arrived—and thus the Continent of Europe has many mammals that we don't have here. True, man, who after all is part of Nature too, has brought a lot across in his boats, and, latterly, in his aeroplanes, and a few of these have escaped and become indigenous.

Of deer, only the Red Deer is truly indigenous. It flourishes best in the Highlands of Scotland where it is hunted with enormous ritual and ceremony by very wealthy people with powerful sporting rifles, who are led up to within sight of the quarry by professional men called gillies. Red deer are also hunted by professional hunters where they are too numerous, and the venison exported to Germany of all places, for the Germans know what is good to eat while the British have forgotten. The Fallow, an import, lives in parks and wild places in many parts of England, and the Roe, secretive little animal that it is, hides in forests and is only seen during the night unless you walk right up on it.

The Sika was introduced into Scotland from Japan in the 1870s and the Muntjac and Chinese Water Deer early this century. There are no wild antelope in Britain, which is a pity. The Europeans have the Chamois and several others. Antelope have horns, deer have antlers, and they are quite different. Antlers are shed once a year and grow again: you are stuck with your horns for life. Conversely in Africa there are hardly any deer: although there is one huge farm in the Karroo (Manor Holme, Middleburgh, Cape Province) on which there is a large herd of very wild Fallow Deer, introduced by John Cecil Rhodes, and now about twice the size of Fallow Deer in England. I once shot one of them. But that is quite by the way.

Of hares there is the Brown and the Blue or Mountain, which turns white in the winter. The rabbit is not indigenous, having been introduced by the silly Normans in the thirteenth century and practically wiped out in 1953 by myxomatosis. This is a disease that has always been enzootic in North America among the Cotton Tails. It probably made them slightly ill when they caught it but didn't kill them and they became immune. Introduced into Australia it nearly exterminated the European Rabbit there (the rabbit had become such a plague in that land of few carnivores that it threatened to destroy the country); a Frenchman introduced it into his estate in France, whence it escaped, spread over Europe, and, inevitably, got

153

across the Channel. Within months south-east England was covered with blind, swollen-headed, crawling, suffering creatures, and the stink of rotting rabbits made it abominable to walk abroad.

But few species have ever been completely wiped out by disease. A few have enough in-built resistance to survive, and these pass their resistance genes to their offspring, and slowly a resistant strain takes over. Meanwhile the disease organism (in this case a virus) is also developing, and more virulent strains are produced, and so there are recurrent epizootics (the non-human equivalent of an epidemic). So our rabbits are slowly coming back—in spite of the efforts of the countryman to prevent them.

There are two sides to the rabbit. Farmers, foresters and growers generally hate him. As much as twenty per cent of a field of corn could be lost to rabbits. The enormous cost of establishing forests in this country pre-myxomatosis was largely due to the cost of fencing, and then completely exterminating the rabbit in the fenced zone. It was just impossible to establish trees where there were rabbits. The rabbit was a source of meat (and a very considerable one) but an inefficient one from man's point of view. Six rabbits ate as much grass as a sheep and a sheep was a far better source of meat than six rabbits.

The farmer and landlord then hated the rabbit, but the poor landless countryman loved him. He was a source of *sport*, for however difficult it may be for the townsman to understand, the countryman has always looked to hunting in one form or another for his entertainment. Also it was the only reliable source of food protein that many a poor countryman had. If he cared to risk arrest by gamekeepers or policemen the countryman could always get a rabbit—and run those risks he had to, for often the health of his children depended on his catching one. The rabbit was often the only meat he could get. The reason, too, why rabbits got out of control in this country was the enormous efforts devoted by the big landowners towards game preservation. They didn't want to preserve the rabbit —they wanted to preserve pheasants, partridges, hares and grouse; but in preserving these they also preserved the rabbit. Their gamekeepers mercilessly hunted and almost completely exterminated the birds and beasts of prey. The 'gamekeepers' gibbet' was a common sight in the countryside when I was a boy: a fence somewhere, strategically placed so that the boss would see it, on which the game-keeper had hung or impaled stoats, weasels, hawks, owls—anything that might conceivably eat the precious game birds or their eggs. The result was that the rabbit lost all his natural enemies. Even man, his arch-enemy, was prevented from hunting him by the gamekeeper—as much as it lay within that potentate's power.

If the rabbit comes back, as come back it will, and if game pre-serving goes on declining and gamekeepers and big landlords become a thing of the past, then the rabbit will take his place among other elements in the balance of nature—not very common, providing people with fun and interest (one pities a generation of children growing up who have never watched baby bunnies scuttering into their holes and stamping their hind feet in alarm), providing the countryman with sport, and people generally with a supply of very good meat. The rabbit only becomes a pest because we let him be-come a pest. If stoats, weasels, polecats and pine martens were allowed to come back, and rabbits too, rabbits would be a very minor problem and beastly and wasteful methods of control such as cyanide gassing and spreading a filthy disease could be forgotten.

There is a small list of other rodents: the ubiquitous House Mouse, made familiar to us all by the works of Beatrix Potter, the Brown Mouse, the Dormouse (made famous by *Alice in Wonderland*), the Edible Dormouse which was introduced at Tring in 1902 and is to be found wild in the Chilterns, whereby it is hoped that the people of the Chilterns will never starve, the Wood Mouse which jumps and builds its nests underground, three Voles, the Water Vole (not found, strangely, in Ireland), the Field and the Bank, and two Rats, the Black, introduced by shipping in the twelfth century and now extinct except in port areas, and the Brown. It was the disease carried by the flea of the Black Rat which nearly exterminated us all with the Plague, but the Brown Rat came and almost exterminated the Black. There are three Shrews, Common, Pygmy and Water, and four Bats.

The indigenous Red Squirrel has nearly been exterminated by the Grey which was imported from America about 1860 and which eats the Red Squirrel's young. The Grey Squirrel does great damage to woods, nipping the growing shoots of the tree out. Campaigns to destroy it have always proved ineffective. If predators such as the pine marten were re-introduced and carefully protected the Grey Squirrel would quickly cease to be a menace. The Hedgehog (called *Hotchi-witchi* by gypsies, who eat them) is ubiquitous and charming.

The Coypu was introduced from South America in the 1930s as a fur farming animal. Inevitably some escaped; it established itself in the Norfolk Broads and has since spread to other watery areas in south-eastern England. It is an animal as large as a collie, although lower to the ground, and has the almost unbelievable characteristic of carrying its teats on its back. I have seen coypu swimming in the Waveney, in the very early morning, with their litters of young hanging on to the teats and being towed through the water like flotillas of destroyers. They look fierce but are not, and are quite good to eat. Their fur is not commercially valuable now but could be if energy and initiative were not lacking. If the fur came to be used again the problem of too many coypu would quickly solve itself. (The popular belief is that the wild coypu have not got such good fur as the captive ones: this is nonsense. I have in my possession some beautiful wild coypu skins.) The government runs a campaign to try to contain them. They are caught, like mink, in long wire cage traps. They are herbivorous, but do some damage to crops (notably sugar beet), to the Norfolk Reed beds by eating the roots of the reeds and making tunnels through them and to river banks by burrowing.

No coypu, as far as I know, has ever migrated as far west as Wales, except one. And that one turned up in the garden of a pub at Abercych, about as far west as you can get, and was killed by the amazed and horrified inn-keeper who thought it was a monstrous rat, and is now stuffed and in a place of honour in the bar. How it got to Abercych no one knows, nor probably ever will.

The Wild Goat (maybe an escape) survives in North Wales and the Western Isles.

Of carnivorous mammals we have the Stoat and Weasel, both small thin-bodied animals that live and hunt down rabbit holes and kill both rats and rabbits. The Stoat is larger and has a black tip to his tail. The Pine Marten still survives, precariously, in Scotland and in Wales and lives in all sorts of woodland—not only pines. I have seen it in oak and ash woodland. The Polecat also still just survives but is very rare. The Badger is another member of this family, although it doesn't look like it because it is fat and stumpy and not long and thin. It is much commoner than most people think: I have seen twenty together on my farm and it is pretty widespread. It makes holes in woodlands, or shares holes with foxes. It does good by eating wasps' nests but harm by rolling on oats and other corn. The latter trait sounds absurd but you have only to lose completely half an acre of hard-won oats by badger-rolling to overcome your scepticism about this habit and many farmers in Wales and other places have had to give up corn-growing owing to this weird and unexplained propensity of badgers to roll on corn. The Wild Cat, or Cat o' Mountain, still exists in the Highlands of Scotland.

The Fox is perhaps the best-known of the larger predators, and is very common and widespread all over the country. The fox is the

natural control of the rabbit. It is notable that when myxomatosis came foxes increased contrary to all expectations. Urban naturalists have expressed surprise at this but every countryman knows the reason. Before 'myxy' rabbits were extensively trapped, both to keep them down and for their meat. Many a farm, in the depression between the wars, was kept going by the sale of rabbits alone. Now the gin-trap, the engine that was used for catching rabbits, also catches foxes. Placed in the entrances of rabbit burrows it was in just the place for doing this, for foxes are always prowling round rabbit burrows. Thus foxes came close to being exterminated in some areas. When 'myxy' came the rabbits went, the gin-trap went, and the foxes came back and are now a major nuisance in remote countrysides where before they were not a nuisance at all. I think they subsist partly on moles. The gin-trap is now illegal, though it is not the law which has got rid of this cruel means of destruction but myxomatosis. No law imposed by city people on country people is ever really enforceable.

The Otter is much commoner than most people think, being very nocturnal and very secretive. Its slides down the banks of rivers and pad-marks can often be seen, but seldom the animal itself. Large fish, such as salmon, with bits bitten out of their shoulders, can often be found lying on the bank. It is arguable that it does more good than harm to fish-stocks by preying, like most predators, on sick and over-aged animals and thus keeping up the health and vigour of the stock and sparing fish food for healthy breeding animals. It almost seems as if herbivores both on land and in water, and indeed some carnivores such as salmon, need a predator to keep them healthy—as witness the awful condition that the rabbits got into on Ramsey Island, off Pembrokeshire, when there were no predators there and before myxomatosis was despicably introduced. Stoats, not myxomatosis, would have been a more humane answer.

The Mink is another escape from fur-farming, and a very dele-terious one. It was first seen wild in the 1930s. Not only does it take a big toll of fish, thus robbing the beautiful and interesting otter, but it slaughters birds, including domestic fowl. I have had a whole chicken-house of hens wiped out in a week. Being slender it can get into nearly anywhere and if a stream runs through a fox-proof chicken-run the fowls are at risk. It is trapped in cage traps but defies efforts at extermination. It is here to stay.

Mammals that have become extinct in Britain in fairly recent centuries are the wolf, possibly not eliminated until the fifteenth century, the bear, wiped out some time before that, the lynx and the beaver. Geraldus Cambrensis noted beavers in the Teifi during his tour of Wales in the thirteenth century. He tells a remarkable story of how they were hunted for their *testicles*, because these were supposedly medicinal. Knowing this the beavers would stop in sight of the pursuing hounds and emasculate themselves so that the huntsmen could pick up the bits they wanted and leave the rest of the animal alone. There were also the wild pig, the wild ox and the wild horse. Wild cattle (the White Park Ox) are still retained in a few parts of the country but how much their blood has been adulterated with domestic ox blood is not known. The Soay Sheep still exists in the Hebrides. I submit that the beaver and the wild pig should be reintroduced. Provided these animals were contained to reasonable numbers by hunting (as the wild pig is in France) they would add interest to our countryside. The Reindeer, once indigenous, has been reintroduced in the Highlands with great success. I would personally like to see a few wolves for it adds to the spice of life to have a few animals large enough and mean enough to attack man, but I might not be able to persuade many people to agree with me: certainly not if they were sheep farmers.

It would be impossible to enumerate the wild birds of the British Isles here, and as there are not hundreds but thousands of books on British birds, and more pour from the presses every year that goes by, it would be ridiculous. Sufficient to mention a few species of importance to the countryman. The Wood Pigeon has, in the past, been a major pest to farmers in England, attacking brassica and clovers in vast flocks. Twenty years ago great shooting drives were organized against them, hundreds of countrymen turning out on the same night with shot guns, and manning every wood and coppice, so that the pigeons, returning home to roost, would have nowhere to take refuge and would pay a toll every time they dropped in to some piece of woodland to perch in the trees. The government provided free ammunition for this purpose. Thousands of birds were shot but the effect on the 'Pigeon Problem' was negligible—there were millions more. Poisoning was tried but given up as dangerous to other species. Thousands fly over from Norway, it is believed, every autumn. But now, for some unexplained reason, pigeon numbers have dramatically decreased and they are no longer anything like such a menace. Maybe this is due to an increase in predators somewhere but nobody seems to know. Birds of prey were nearly wiped out in England by various poisons that became much used on the land in the 1940s and 50s and this may have led to the plague of pigeons. Now the government is exercising at least some control over these poisons. Birds of prey suffered more than graminivorous birds because there is a build-up of poisons as you go up the food-chain and hawks, and owls and falcons nearly became extinct.

Gamekeepers too caused serious imbalance of nature, and still do wherever they operate. Game-preserving encourages rodents enormously for example, for all the predators of rodents are also predators of the pheasant. No gamekeeper can ever be persuaded to suffer a predator of any sort to live, no matter how enlightened his boss is. Fortunately gamekeepers are well on the way to becoming an extinct species themselves.

Countrymen have mixed feelings about Rooks, Crows and Jackdaws. These birds eat seed corn, knock down ripe corn in the field to peck out the grain, and make a mess of sheaves of corn set up in stooks. The old saying when planting seed was:

One for the Rook, one for the Crow
One to rot, and one to grow.

On the other hand these birds eat wire-worm and leather-jackets, and other soil pests, and no countryman would ever want to see them extinct. Rooks are traditionally thinned out by shooting the squabs, or immature birds, during that short period when they are leaving the nests in the rookery, hopping about on the branches, but cannot fly. At this stage they make a very good pie.

The lack of predators in Britain, and the fact that the Briton does not normally shoot song-birds, makes the growing of various kinds of fruit very difficult. Cherries can be grown successfully only in large orchards, where there are too many cherries for the birds to eat, or with constant vigilance to keep birds away. Outdoor grapes, for the same reason, are very difficult. In France and Italy there is no such trouble: but in those countries bands of heavily armed men, slung about with cartridge belts like South American film bandits, and carrying large shotguns, stalk the lanes, scorning not to blast into eternity even the robin or the wren. Most of us in this country would rather have the song-birds even if we have to do without the fruit, but surely there could be a compromise somewhere along the line. More Sparrow Hawks might be a good one. Fortunately the latter bird, and the Kestrel, are making a small come-back owing to one new development of man. The verges of the new motorways are proving very attractive to them. No gamekeepers prowl along these avenues.

We will now deal with the activities engaged in by countrymen connected with wild animals and birds. Many of these consist of hunting and killing, and the very mention of them excites strong passions in urban breasts, but I am describing them here because they exist, and are part of country living, and the fact that I describe them does not mean that I necessarily condone them.

Fox-hunting arouses perhaps the strongest passions, but there are two very different and quite distinct forms of this particular branch of venery. In lowland Britain fox-hunting is carried out by a mixture of country people and townspeople, all riding horses (in theory at least—for every follower on a horse now there are two in motor cars), some of them dressed up in special garments, and with a large pack of hounds, the latter under the control of the Huntsman, sometimes an amateur but sometimes a hunt servant, the people under the control (or *not* under the control) of the Master, always an amateur and, in hunt circles, a very important gentleman. Very often he is Master because he has a lot of money some of which goes to supporting all those hounds.

Before the invention of the breech-loading gun, the gin-trap and effective poisons, hunting with hounds was by far the most effective way of keeping down foxes, as it was wolves, deer, otters, hares, and many another animal that could be, uncontrolled, a nuisance to man. The pack of hounds was then a most important tool of the countryside, and the Squire, who generally owned it, was performing a real service. Now, in lowland Britain, a pack of hounds is a luxury, kept for sport, and probably if hunting was 'abolished' the fox would rapidly become extinct (except in the big cities where it has recently started to establish itself). Poison baits and gases would quickly eliminate it.

In highland Britain, however, particularly in Wales and the Lake District, what is known as the Farmers' Pack is an essential part of the economy. A Farmers' Pack consists of maybe twenty couple

161

(hounds are counted in couples—thus forty-one hounds is called 'twenty-and-a-half couple'), fed and looked after by a full-time Huntsman paid by the local farmers, a van to carry them in, and perhaps a hundred stalwart mountain farmers, each with a shotgun, and also mounted, nowadays, in vans and motor cars. The Field (the huntsman's term for the people engaged in the hunt) ring a wood, or piece of forestry plantation, high up in the mountains, each man standing within shot-gun range of his neighbour. The hounds are 'cast' into the wood by the Huntsman, who is the only person there wearing special clothes (maybe a green jacket and breeches, a huntsman's cap and carrying a long whip and a horn). The hounds either kill as many foxes as they can in the wood or chase them out where they get shot by the guns. A few terriers are carried to chase out any foxes that have 'gone to earth' (gone down a hole). Spades are also carried to dig the terriers out if they stay down there. A dozen foxes may thus be destroyed in a day, a hundred or two in a winter season. The lamb crop in such country (the number of lambs which manage to survive to grow into big sheep) is entirely dependent on the fox kill. The mountain farmers give up a great deal of time to this pursuit, and take turns at keeping puppies and larger hounds on their farms during the close season, and put their hands in their pockets to feed the pack and pay the Huntsman, but they do it willingly because they know that they cannot farm without it. I lost three lambs to foxes last year from my tiny flock and a neighbour lost eleven: quite a substantial part of his income. We don't have a Farmers' Pack here and I wish we did.

Other packs of hounds in this country are kept for hunting otters, red deer, and hares. Otter-hunting is strongly attacked on the grounds that the otter is rare, and that it is inhumane to hunt mammals in the summer when they have young. (Otters have young all the year round as a matter of fact.) Otter-hunting is conducted in the summer and not in the winter. When a bitch otter is killed it may well be that her young may starve to death. Personally I would like to see otter packs turned to hunting coypu, but that might just be a silly suggestion. As things are, huntsmen spend a lot of time whipping hounds away from coypu. Otter-hunting is, I regret to say, very interesting and can be very good fun. I don't think that some people should legislate about other people's fun, but it might be that otter-hunting will die away because the hunters themselves turn against it for humanitarian reasons. If the otter ever *did* become a nuisance in this country, as it might (not having any predator to control it except man) then probably hunting with hounds is as good a way of controlling it as any other. When freshwater fish was an important source of food for man, as it was in the Middle Ages, then there was every excuse for eliminating some of the otters but not, of course, all of them.

The Red Deer stag is hunted on Exmoor and Dartmoor and this again arouses strong passions. Often as many 'antis' (anti-blood-sports enthusiasts) are hunting the hunters as hunters are hunting the stag. Deer can be controlled very humanely and effectively with the rifle, and there is no ecological or economic argument for hunting them with hounds—the only argument in favour of doing it is that it is fun. It is arguable that deer have been evolved over millennia to escape from pursuers and there is nothing much wrong in making them do it from time to time.

red deer

roe deer

fallow deer

Red Deer are shot in the Highlands by sportsmen, who often pay large sums for the privilege. The sportsmen are led up within shot of the deer by professional gillies, a stag is pointed out to them, and they are told to shoot it. They shoot it. If they miss, the gillie probably shoots it. This is a very humane method of controlling deer. But more and more Red Deer in the Highlands, and Reindeer also, are being cropped by professional hunters, in order not only to control their numbers but also to get saleable meat. In a country with no predators except man it is necessary to control the numbers of herbivores otherwise these will either spread on to farmland and push out man himself, or else, fenced in, will breed up to the point when they will begin to suffer hunger, be thin and miserable, and many will starve. Nothing is more unhappy than the members of a species which has nothing to control its numbers except the food supply. Also, venison is very good meat, and the Red Deer may well be a better way of converting the herbage of high mountains into human food than are sheep.

In the lowlands all the deer have to be controlled, and are, by shooting. The Forestry Commission, in particular, employs special men to do it; they watch the deer very closely, and only shoot sick or very old specimens, or healthy ones that are seen to be doing damage, or if the stock of deer in a forest is getting very numerous. If the deer in a forestry plantation get too numerous they soon begin to invade surrounding farmland and there are complaints, and they also do a certain amount of damage to the trees. In fact if they are too numerous the trees cannot be established at all. As a Scottish forester once said to me, about Roe Deer, 'They are verra seveere on the trrees.' Roe deer, in particular, have a peculiar habit of 'sharpening their antlers' on trees and thus barking them and killing them.

Hares are hunted by people on horseback with packs of hounds called harriers, and by people on foot with packs of beagles. The latter activity can be as exhausting to the hounds and the people as to the hares, and for every hare killed twenty get away. As a device for making you *run* large distances over rough country, there is nothing like beagling except possibly being chased by a bull.

Coursing is the art of catching and killing hares with greyhounds, or other dogs like them. It is quite different from pack-hunting in that the dogs hunt entirely by sight and not by scent. Fox-hounds or beagles hunt with their noses close to the ground and only lift them when the scent is in the air or they can see the quarry. Greyhounds seldom use their noses and you will see them leaping up high above long grass in order to be able to catch a glimpse of an otherwise invisible quarry. Whippets are like miniature greyhounds and will sometimes kill a hare though generally they are not quite fast enough. They were bred by colliers and other industrial workers to provide sport by racing. Their owners will stand in a line, the dogs held at a distance by helpers, released all together at a signal, whereupon the owners madly wave handkerchiefs and shout to their favourite animals. There is much betting.

Lurchers are generally greyhounds crossed with something else. Crosses are various, sometimes a sheepdog bitch put in pup to a greyhound will throw a good lurcher, sometimes rough-coated deerhounds are crossed with a greyhound bitch: the aim is to produce a dog with the speed of a greyhound but with a rough coat and more sense. Gypsies are great lurcher-breeders and will pay high prices for good ones. The lurcher is the poacher's dog. It is silent, will keep out of sight of strangers, will bring game back to hand, and I have known a lurcher trained to run home secretly at a whistle from his master. An intelligent lurcher will cut corners when chasing a hare, anticipate a hare's movements, and often bring her down. But if he doesn't do it within five minutes he probably won't do it at all for he will be too exhausted, and it is a good lurcher that can run again without several hours to recover though I had one that did, on occasion, run down and kill three hares in a day. He was exceptional. Lurchers will also sometimes pin a pheasant if they can come up on one on the ground, and some are good with rabbits.

Shooting is done either with the rifle or the shotgun. To consider the latter first: a shotgun has a smooth-bored barrel, quite large, and fires not one projectile but a number of small shot, generally lead. It has a comparatively short range, not more than thirty to seventy yards, depending on what sort of gun it is, what sort of ammunition, and what sort of quarry, but as the shot spreads out it makes a 'pattern' that is big enough to take in a quarry even if the gun is not aimed right at it. A rifle of course has a *rifled* barrel (that is spiral grooves are cut in it) and fires only one projectile which is called a bullet. The bullet, being of soft metal, is cut into by the spiral *lands* inside the barrel (the grooves are called *furrows*, the high places between them *lands*) and caused to spin. It is this spinning motion that keeps the bullet going straight—if it were not spinning it would turn or pitch-pole in the air and then go off its course. It has a much greater range than a shotgun, can be accurately aimed either by open, aperture, or telescopic sights; a medium rifle (say a 7-millimetre) will kill a stag at half a mile (it would at a mile if you could hit it) and a 'two-two' (.22 inch bore), which is almost a toy rifle, will kill a rabbit or a hare at a hundred yards if you aim it straight. When people talk of a gun in this country they almost invariably mean a shotgun. Nearly every countryman has one, they require a licence and nowadays a permit but the permits are nothing like so hard to get as rifle permits.

Rifle-shooting is confined to stags in the Highlands, deer-control in the Lowlands, and a few people shoot rabbits, foxes, and other small game and vermin with 'two-twos'. It is very difficult to hit a flying or fast-moving object with a rifle.

Shotguns are used for a great many purposes. The two main ways of shooting animals or birds with a shotgun are—driving and walking-up. Walking-up consists of one person or a number of people in a line walking over ground that is likely to hold game and shooting the game they want to as it takes to the air or runs away. Very few Britons (should one say this with a throb of pride? Or not?) will shoot a stationary animal with a shotgun or a bird on the ground.

Driving consists of having a line of beaters walking towards the 'guns' (the word in this sense means the men with the guns) to drive birds or ground game towards them, whereupon the game is shot. Sometimes thousands of pheasants are shot in a day like this, and a landowner's standing among his peers is often dependent on how many pheasants he can 'show' in a day's beating. Some of the sportsmen have two guns and a loader, the latter a man who loads one gun while his master is shooting with the other. Most shotguns used in this country are double-barrelled, usually with two barrels side by side or, less usually, 'over-and-under'—with one barrel over the other. Each barrel is fired by its own trigger. To shoot two birds with

two shots one after the other is thus called 'getting a right-and-left'.
Impoverished people, such as the author, have single-barrelled shotguns, but such people do not adorn big pheasant drives. We 'shoot
for the pot' or to destroy vermin which is attacking our crops.

pheasants

partridge

grouse

Partridges, both the English variety and the red-legged 'Frenchman' are also shot, either by 'walking-up' or by driving over the guns
by beaters. It takes some skill to shoot them for they fly very low and
fast. They are becoming rare because of chemicals on the land which
destroy their feed. Snipe are small birds which feed on marshy
ground, and are shot for sport as well as food. They are the hardest
quarry of all to hit, having a strange, sudden, zigzag flight and take
off at one's feet like rockets. Woodcock are related, found in woods
in winter (they are migratory, like snipe) and are also hard to hit,
being silent and ghost-like and suddenly away.

Grouse live on hills and feed on young heather, and shooting
them, in big drives, is big business in the North of England and
Scotland. Sportsmen pay great prices for the right to shoot. Black
Game and Capercaillie are rarer, on high mountains, the latter as big
as a heavy hen.

Wildfowlers are a race apart. They shoot wild duck of various
sorts, wild geese, and such wading birds as are allowed to be shot by
law. Most wading birds are now protected, but that doesn't stop
them being very good to eat. Wildfowlers therefore generally shoot
in wet places, on the saltings by the sea, in estuaries, along big rivers,

or by lakes. All water-birds tend to 'flight' in the evening, and again at dawn, and it is at those times that 'flighters' will go and wait for them, crouching behind sea walls or hiding in holes and ditches. The birds generally flight when it is almost dark, and come very fast, and you have to have great knowledge to know just where they will come, and the successful flighter has to be very skilful. Estuary and sea-birds also flight at various stages of the tide, often at night, and many a wildfowler spends night after freezing night, in the winter when his sport is at its best, hiding up for birds to fly off the mud-flats perhaps, when the rising tide covers them.

Punting is a sport seldom practised now (although it still is in one or two places). It was once a profession, and many a fisherman, who could not fish in the gales of winter, eked out his living by keeping a gun-punt. The punt is long and narrow and very low in the water, and has a big gun—almost a cannon—mounted on its fore-deck. The punter rowed the punt out, generally at night or in thick fog, until he heard birds in front of him, then he lay down in the punt on his belly and propelled the punt forward with 'setting sticks' if the water was shallow, or 'paddles' if deeper. When he felt he was near enough to the birds—provided they didn't see or hear him first—he would fire the gun by means of a lanyard (piece of cord) attached to the trigger. There would be a blinding flash and a terrible roar as the great gun went off, often firing a pound of shot or more, the punt would be shot backwards in the water by the recoil, and the punter would row quickly up to pick up his birds. Twenty or thirty wild geese, forty widgeon or other wild ducks, or teal, were not uncommon bags and one man on the Essex Blackwater once mowed down over *four hundred* knot and dunlin in one shot. Strangely, in those days of professional wildfowlers, there were many more wildfowl than there are now. I remember on the Hamford Water and the Blackwater the horizon being blanked-out by great flocks of knot and dunlin, huge companies of Brent and Barnacle Geese honked out on the estuaries, and thousands of widgeon flew over our heads at every flight. Now, in spite of large areas of protected water and land, these birds are very scarce indeed. Some other factor beside the gun must have reduced them.

As for the countrymen and the fish of the lakes and rivers,

legitimate fishing is apt to be an urban sport. Wealthy city people hire stretches of river, or lake shore, to catch 'game fish' meaning trout, grayling, sea-trout or sewern, and salmon. These fish are generally taken with artificial flies, either 'wet flies' or 'dry flies'. The former, usually used in fast-running water, are dragged through

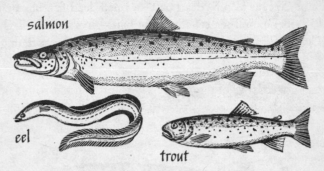

salmon

eel

trout

the water; the latter delicately cast, with great skill, so as to land on top of the water and be kept there by surface tension. Very light line is used so that when the fish takes the fly and is 'struck' (i.e. the line is pulled taught to drive the hook home), the fish has to be skilfully fought to bring it to the bank without the line breaking. Worms can be used for trout in some places, but their use is considered by some people to be 'unsporting'. Spoons, and other flashing lures, are also often used.

As opposed to game fish, Roach, Perch, Tench, Carp, Pike and

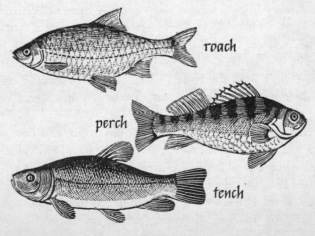

roach

perch

tench

Bream are *coarse fish*. While game fish are generally fished for in the summer, coarse fish are more often taken in the winter. Although fly will sometimes take some coarse fish, worms, maggots (called by anglers 'gentles') and even bits of dough or bread, are more often used. Spoons or other moving lures are used for the carnivores such as Perch or Pike, as also is 'dead bait' (a small dead fish impaled in a hooked device) or, rather cruelly, 'live bait'—live fish similarly impaled. Coarse fishing may seem a more proletarian sport than game,

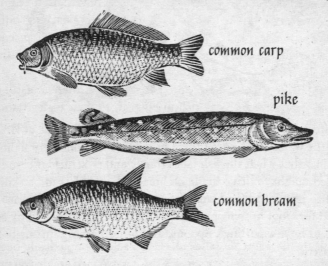

common carp

pike

common bream

and all through the winter thousands of city working men come out into the country in busloads, accompanied by cases of bottled beer, to sit in serried ranks along the banks of rivers or canals, to catch coarse fish, solemnly weigh them, and put them, alive, back in the water again. Sheffield is the biggest centre of this sport and that city, one would think from the river banks, must be practically emptied every winter weekend. Large sums of money are wagered on the biggest catch.

The countryman, after plenty of bent-pin fishing as a boy, generally loses interest in coarse fishing, although the odd individual here and there makes a good tax-free income catching eels, which sell for a good price. Eels are taken on long-lines (lines with many hooks on them), eel hives (basket-work or wire-netted box traps), nets of various sorts, by 'babbing' (lowering bunches of worms threaded on wool yarn to the bottom—the eels get their teeth caught in the woollen yarn), or *pritching*. The latter method is stabbing the mud of ditches with a sort of barbed Neptune's trident.

Game fishing for many a countryman means poaching, generally for salmon, which sell, currently, for over a pound a pound. They are taken by the gaff, with the aid of a torch at night or sharp eyes by day, various nets, or, unforgivably and generally by city poachers, with lime, cyanide or explosives. The true country poacher will never use these indiscriminate methods—he does not want to ruin his pitch. An army of river bailiffs tries to stop the poaching but the poachers catch far more salmon than the bailiffs catch poachers. When a poacher is caught he is heavily fined, and must poach thereafter all the harder to make the money to pay his fines.

On the Rivers Teifi, Towi and Taf, in Wales, there are still professional coracle men. They fish in pairs from their craft of ancient design, two men in coracles drifting slowly downstream towing a light net between them. When a fish swims into the net it is entangled, hauled to one of the coracles, and hit on the head with a *priest*. This is the name given to a small boxwood club. It delivers the last rites. Both net and coracle are of a design of such antiquity that they go back to Neolithic times. It is sad that at the moment angling interests are trying hard to drive the coracles off the rivers. A fight is being made to save them (after all the coracle has practically become the emblem of Wales!). Of course if the coracle men are driven out of their coracles they will merely turn to other, and more destructive, forms of poaching, so no interests will be served. In any case, as the Teifi coracle men point out, fifty years ago when there were fifty coracle licences at Cilgerran alone, there were far more salmon than there are now. It is not the coracles that are depleting the fishery. Unfortunately the Danes have discovered the feeding grounds of the salmon in the West Atlantic and are netting them on a huge scale. They have been persuaded to restrict somewhat their depredations but if other nations, notably the Japanese, get into this fishery it will be the end of the Atlantic Salmon for all time.

Another licensed salmon fishery is draw-netting, or seine-netting, in estuaries and the mouths of rivers. Generally licences are limited to a small number, and often they go down from father to son, and here again great efforts are being made to eliminate them altogether. It is notable, though, that in rivers where there is a great deal of netting, such as the Tweed, there are also plenty of salmon. The fact is that it only takes one hen salmon to get up to her spawning ground to lay an awful lot of eggs.

Chapter 10

Plants and Trees of the Countryside

Hooker's *Student's Flora* lists one thousand, three hundred species of plants in Britain. Druce's *British Plant List*, which includes casuals, lists four thousand, two hundred and fifty. Anyway, enough to deter the present writer from embarking on a description of wild plants, and in any case books on wild plants proliferate as fast as books about birds—dozens come out every year. The countryman is surprisingly little affected by wild plants other than trees and the weeds that he has to get rid of. Some countrywomen make wine out of certain flowers, for example cowslips and dandelions; nettles are used for wine and beer, and for flavouring real (malt) beer, and boiled when young for 'spinach'; Fat Hen, or Good King Henry, a rampant annual weed of arable land, is also much used for spinach; and a few country people here and there still gather medicinal herbs. In fact there is a small, but very secretive and little-known industry of gathering such plants as fox-gloves and mandrake to supply the pharmaceutical trade.

Trees, however, are of prime importance to the countryman, at least in such areas from which they have not been eliminated by modern farming methods.

Trees, like other plants and wild animals, returned to Britain after the last Ice Age, but before the land bridge with the Continent was cut by the sea. The study of pollen, which has been preserved in peat bogs, has given us a pretty good picture of the successive invasions of trees after the ice went.

Birch, being extremely frost-hardy, was the first tree to invade—

probably a dwarf species at first such as we still find today on the northern tree-line of Europe. The Scots Pine followed, first growing with the Birch, then partially eliminating it from large areas. Oak, Hazel, and Alder in the wet places, came next, then Beech on calcareous, or limey soils. Beech shades out all rivals, except the Yew, also an early arrival, and one which can stand dense shade. Ash came in to colonize calcareous soils too, notably the Magnesium

Limestones and Carboniferous Limestones of the north and west. The Lime, or Linden, was an indigenous tree here, although it practically died out and had to be re-introduced by man. The Holly was also an early arrival. Substantially, the above short list comprises all the trees that were widespread in Britain before the Channel bridge was cut.

When man came he had to avoid the forests, except for hunting and foraging grounds, until the invention of bronze made it possible for him to clear the forest and till. Stone Age man was perfectly capable of cutting down trees with his stone axes (experiments in Denmark have shown these to be very effective), but it was the *hoe* (not the plough as is popularly supposed) that enabled the forests to be cultivated, and this had to wait until the Bronze Age. The technique of clearing and cultivating forests in England must have been the same as *chena* cultivation now in the northern jungles of Sri Lanka, or the denser savanna country of Central Africa. The trees were cut down but not stumped. The wood was burned. The ground between the stumps was hoed, or mattocked. Crops were grown— very successfully at first, for the old forest floor was rich in humus

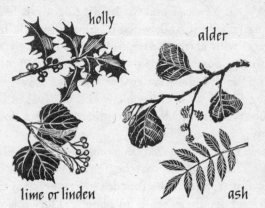

holly

alder

lime or linden

ash

and the potash from burnt timber, and there were none of the weeds of arable land. After a decade or two though the latter came in, Couch Grass and Ground Elder became a nuisance, the fertility was used up, and so the cultivators moved on to another piece of forest. In due course the forest they had left behind grew again, and the fertility was replenished.

With the Iron Age, and particularly the arrival of the Belgian Celts in about 50 B.C., it was possible to conquer the forest lands more permanently. The plough cannot, of course, work on land which has not been stumped. Only hand cultivation (the hoe or mattock) can tackle that. But the new Celts not only cut down the trees but stumped the land, and they could use their heavy wheeled ploughs, pulled by long teams of oxen, to keep the forest from coming back. When the English arrived this process went on, but much faster.

The forests began to give way before the axe and the plough. As the population of each village increased so more land was cleared and taken into the strip system. In a country such as England there was

175

more than enough hard timber for every possible need, for England was one great forest, except for the hills and mountains, before man cut it down. But man's need for timber increased, for he used it for house-building, firewood, ship-building, and every other purpose, and—as time went on—more and more for iron-smelting. Before the invention of coke-smelting all iron, and in fact all metal, had to be smelted with charcoal. Charcoal is wood that has been burnt with insufficient oxygen. You can make it by digging a pit, filling it with wood, setting light to it, and, when it is burning well, burying the burning wood with earth. Better, you can build a pyre of wood, cover it with clay except for air holes at the top and bottom, fire it, then bung up the air holes. Charcoal was used for many purposes: in fact anything for which later people would use coal or coke. Glass furnaces, blast furnaces, blooming furnaces, forges, foundry furnaces—all were fired with charcoal.

It has often been written that 'iron-smelting destroyed the forests of England'. This is not strictly true, for trees were not clear-felled for smelting but *coppiced*. The practice of coppicing is to cut large trees down and let them send up shoots. Thus a young sweet chestnut tree, for example, can be felled, the stump will send up perhaps half a dozen shoots, these will grow into a thick clump, and after from seven to twenty years (depending on soil, and the use of the timber) can be cut again. More shoots will grow up and these can be cut again. Some coppice is hundreds of years old. The iron smelters and founders coppiced the forests, cutting over the same forest again and again, and, provided they had enough forest to work over, established a self-renewing husbandry.

Pollarding is another technique for the continuous production of timber. In this case the original trees are cut six feet above the ground and allowed to shoot up from there. The reason for this is that the growing shoots are out of the reach of grazing animals. Coppiced woods must be kept fairly clear of grazers at least until the new growth is strong enough to withstand them. In England there are hardly any wild, self-sown, indigenous trees which are not deformed by coppicing or pollarding. Nearly all the old oaks in the New Forest, Epping, Dean, and Wyre, for example, have been pollarded, probably again and again. Oak, Beech, and Willow are commonly pollarded: Hazel, Hornbeam, Sweet Chestnut, Oak, Birch, Alder and Ash can be coppiced. Softwoods, in fact all conifers, are unsuitable for either of these techniques.

But at least by 1483 enough forest had been cleared in England to cause Edward IV to pass a statute authorizing lords of the manor to enclose woods for seven years after cutting. This was to keep grazing

pollarded willows

animals and the plough out long enough to allow time for regrowth of woodland. In Tudor times the use of timber for all purposes increased enormously and people began to get seriously worried about the supply. In 1664 John Evelyn wrote his *Silva*, in which he made an impassioned plea for landowners to plant forests. This followed a famous lecture he gave to the newly-formed Royal Society on 15 October 1662. 'We had better be without gold than without timber', was his message. The growing Navy demanded more and more oak, elm and beech. Oak 'crooks' are needed in plenty in ship-building: branches grown into natural curves, for the curving frames ('ribs' to the landlubber), knees, stems, stern-posts and aprons, of a ship should all be built out of naturally curving timber. For crooks oaks growing in the open were needed, such as park oaks, or standard oaks in coppice: oak with plenty of twisty branches. 'Coppice-with-standards' is still to be seen in southern England: generally sweet chestnut coppice with oak trees towering above it at intervals. The coppice is cut down every dozen or so years, the standards perhaps once a century. The idea arose from the need to have wide spreading oaks which would grow many crooked branches. Nowadays long straight oaks are needed for sawing into straight planks and standards are unpopular, as are park trees. Crooks are no longer needed, but maybe one day they will be again.

Coppice is still grown in Kent and Sussex, largely for hop-poles but also for chestnut paling, hurdles, and other purposes. Land-owners auction the woodland off in sections called *cants*, *moots* or *stools* according to the area. According to the area too, standards (the big trees standing up over the coppice) are called *stores*, *staddles*, *standils*, *tellers*, *reserves* or *princes*. (Language in the country is infinitely variable.)

Another big use of timber in days gone by, but not so much now, was tannin. The bark of oak, birch and alder was used for this, the trees being felled in the spring, for only then would the bark 'run'— i.e. come off easily when ripped with a sharp spade or a draw knife. Even today some scrub oak is felled for this purpose: notably on the banks of the Fal, in Cornwall. The bark was milled at the tannery, in other words ground up, soaked in water, and the hides were then immersed in a weak solution of the tannin, to be transferred into progressively stronger solutions, and after in some cases up to a year, the leather was tanned. Other chemical means are now used but the leather is nothing like so good.

After John Evelyn's *Silva*, English landlords began to plant trees, and by the beginning of the eighteenth century the tree-planting craze had taken hold. All through the eighteen- and nineteen-hundreds big landlords planted trees, mostly hardwoods: oak, beech, lime, sycamore, horse chestnut, sweet chestnut, and many exotic varieties. We owe what is left of the beauty of our countryside to this fact. Planting fell off after the repeal of the Corn Laws, for landowners did not have as much money, nor incentive to develop their estates; and by the beginning of the twentieth century planting was sporadic indeed. The First World War devastated our forests, parks and woodlands. By then the country had become completely dependent on imported softwoods, and this supply was cut off by the U-boats. The British Isles were ravaged for timber: an army of lumberjacks was recruited in Canada to come over and help cut it. In four years much of the planting of two centuries was felled.

After the First World War the government decided to guard against another timber blockade by extensive planting, but had not the courage to plant hardwood trees: after all, four years is the term of office of a government—so how can any party in power trade present wealth and convenience for future benefits? It is amazing that our democratic society did indeed pluck up enough courage and belief in the future to plant any trees at all. In 1919 the Forestry Commission was set up, land was purchased in large blocks all over the country—mostly marginal land or land that was not very much good for farming—and planted with conifers. Now the Forestry Commission has 1,212,000 hectares of forest, or 3,030,000 acres. With few exceptions the trees they have planted are conifers: largely Scots Pine and Corsican Pine in the dry south-east and Sitka Spruce in the wetter north and west; but quite a wide range of other conifers has been planted. The choice of species has been limited by the fact that for the most part the Commission only acquired marginal land: either fairly unproductive mountain land or very light or sandy soil in the Lowlands such as the Brecklands and Sandlings of East Anglia, and also because the Commission's brief has been to produce timber as quickly as possible. Opinions differ as to whether it was desirable to cover huge areas of mountainside with rows and rows of conifers. Most of the land was bought by the Commission during the Depression of the twenties and thirties, when no farmer could make a decent living, and sheep farmers in the hills were very willing to get a few pounds an acre for their land and thereafter get jobs working for 'The Forestry'. But after the initial clearings, and fencings, and rabbit-clearance, and plantings, and then the first thinning (at about seven years), the labour require-ments of a forest drop off, and in fact there is very little work to do for perhaps twenty years, when there may be a second thinning, and then nothing to do for another forty years, when the final clear-felling takes place. Thus the spate of employment fell away, sheep and wool prices improved, and erstwhile sheep farmers found them-selves out of a job, without their old sheep ranges, or with them very much reduced, and the Commission lost popularity. The Commission has always urged the economies of scale in planting: it costs less per acre to fence, for example, or to serve with roads, a ten-thousand-acre block than it does a thousand-acre block; but perhaps a better course would have been to have sacrificed some economy of scale in order to have had smaller belts of forest, spread more evenly about the country, so that all areas would have benefited by tree-planting, but no area been overwhelmed by it. Maybe (one hopes) this will be the pattern of the future. Certainly *no* farm in the land should be without tree-planting.

The government has helped individual farmers and landowners to plant trees by high subsidies, help and advice, and, until recently, by substantial tax reliefs. The result of this policy has been entirely beneficial—it has meant a multitude of small woodlands being established about the countryside, considerable planting of hard-woods besides conifers, because private planters are not always content to suffer the monotony of nothing but conifers, and there is now a total of about two million hectares (five million acres) of forest in Great Britain. Unfortunately in 1974 ('National Tree Year') the government saw fit to end tax-reliefs on tree-planting, and also subsidies, and so future generations will suffer as a consequence.

As for the 'serried ranks of conifers'—surely any trees are better than no trees, and the 'serried ranks' look a lot better, and more part of the natural scene, after about twenty years, when the ranks have been broken by thinning. It is only sad that the kind of organic forestry that can be seen practised in Germany cannot also be practised in Britain. This is the management of a mixed-species forest, with diverse age-groups, continuous felling as trees become ripe, and natural regeneration from seed. Properly managed, such a forest can be extremely productive, is very beautiful, and will shelter and feed a great variety of species of plant and animal life. But such management takes a kind of skill, sympathy, and instinct which cannot fairly be looked for in run-of-the-mill foresters.

Another reason for the 'all-conifers' policy is that, as the general quality of life deteriorates, hardwoods are no longer required in any quantity. Furniture is now made of the cheapest of softwoods, covered perhaps with thin hardwood veneer. Softwood is needed in enormous quantity to be pulped and made into the various kinds of 'chip-board' and 'hard-board' that more and more of our buildings are made of, or for the roofing- and floor-timbers of the millions of new houses that have to be built to house a growing population. The idea of using *oak* for house-timbering, as our ancestors did, is now unthinkable.

The cost of establishing timber has been greatly reduced, incidentally, by myxomatosis. Before this, land had to be rabbit-fenced—in itself a costly operation—and thereafter cleared of the very last rabbit. If there was one pair of rabbits left, or one doe in kid, the whole operation was rendered useless for the rabbits would breed to cover the area again in one summer. After the initial clearance constant patrolling by warreners was necessary, to ensure that the fences remained completely rabbit-proof, and to destroy any rabbit that did get in. A gate left open might do enormous harm. But now one only needs to fence against farm stock, and maybe keep deer under reasonable control, to establish a plant.

Conifers are normally planted, with the spade, at one thousand, seven hundred and fifty trees to the acre. They are planted very close together so that they grow straight and tall—racing each other to the sky. They are thinned maybe twice or three times before the final felling, and when that occurs there will be perhaps only two hundred and fifty trees left. Conifers may be sixty or seventy years old when clear-felled—oak must be perhaps a hundred and twenty. The first thinnings of softwoods may go for pit-props down coal-mines, or more and more nowadays for pulping. They may also be pressure-creosoted and used for fence stakes but they have a very short life. It will be seen that, as the first big plantings of the Forestry Commission were not until about 1930, it will be another twenty years before widespread harvesting of mature timber will begin in this country. After this there should be a fairly constant supply, as of course land will be replanted as soon as clear-felled.

The countryman, unless he works in forestry or buys softwood timber from a timber merchant, is not much interested in conifers. True, larch makes quite durable fence-posts or gate-posts if it is impregnated with creosote, but other softwoods have little use on farms or cottage gardens. Hardwoods, however, are of interest to him, and we might discuss some of the uses of a few of them.

Alder is a poor wood, and many countrymen look upon alder as nothing more than a weed. It grows along river banks and in wet places and is very widespread, pushing out better trees. It makes poor firewood unless thoroughly dry, when it burns quickly without much heat. It is fairly durable under water and can be used for revetting streams or ponds. Its main use, in the past, was clog soles. Clogs were widely worn in Wales and the North of England until the last ten years or so (a few still are, by sensible people) and the soles were almost invariably made of alder. Gangs of men used to travel from alder coppice to coppice, living in rough shelters, felling the coppiced trees and cutting them into clog soles. English and Welsh clogs, unlike most Dutch ones, had wooden soles but leather uppers. Other uses for alder which still exist are for brush backs, hat blocks, and cotton reels.

Ash is the queen of trees (as Oak is the king). As fuel it is supreme:

> Ash, sear or green
> Is fuel for a queen.

Ash is the toughest of our woods—springy and resilient. Cart shafts, the felloes of wheels, tool handles, hames for horse collars, oars, paddles, tennis rackets, hockey sticks and when aeroplanes were made out of wood, ash was the wood. It is inclined to rot if left damp and isn't much good for fencing posts on this account but it makes good gates and hurdles. It *cleaves* easily (splits along the grain) and the cleft ash is the most usual wood for sheep hurdles and small gates or hurdle-gates. Professional craftsmen bury ash for several months before using it, as this allows it to season sufficiently protected from Ash Beetle which would otherwise bore into it. Creosoting deters the beetle as well. Kept creosoted, and not in contact with the ground or long grass, ash gates will last for decades—but not as long as either oak or split chestnut.

Beech is the great wood for furniture-making—being white and clean-grained, it will cleave. Men called *bodgers* work out in the beechwoods all the year, working in the open or in rough shelters (called hovels), felling the beech, cleaving the big trunks and working the small wood in the round. They turn chair-legs on primitive but very effective foot-driven lathes. The beech woods in which they work are not clear-felled, but the mature trees only are cut down every year, thus allowing the next generation of trees to grow out and expand, and leaving space for seedlings to survive. Woods so managed produce more timber per acre than woods clear-felled, with far less labour; they are more beautiful, and less prone to disease. Beech is fine for wood-carving, tent and clothes pegs, butchers' blocks and turnery of all sorts. The word beech comes from the German *buche*, and so does our word book. The connection is that beech boards were used for the covers of books in ancient times.

Birch is a much better wood than most people think it is. In the Highlands of Scotland it was once used for everything timber can be used for. Seasoned and then creosoted it makes good fencing stakes. Its twigs, when not used for beating boys, were extensively made into brooms by men called *broom squires*. The compressed heads of the besoms were bound with fibres made from hammered ash poles, peeled brambles, willow twigs, twisted hazel, bast from lime trees, or even thinly riven oak or chestnut. When dried it makes a very hot-burning firewood. It turns well and tons of it are used for making cotton reels, etc.

Chestnut (Sweet, not Horse). This is the most useful wood of all for the farmer or estate manager. It lasts in the ground, as poles or gate-posts, as long as heart of oak, without any treatment. It cleaves readily—more readily than oak. It makes barrel staves, ladder rungs, hurdles (heavier but more durable than ash). It is grown in all the hop-growing areas for hop poles. It is very fast-growing and coppices marvellously. If ever our countryside returns or moves forward to a higher level of regional self-sufficiency, sweet chestnut coppice should be established wherever it will grow, and become the most widely planted of our trees. The coppice is auctioned, when ripe (i.e. about twelve years after it was last cut) in *cants* (as we have seen) of several acres, to the cleavers, who cut and cleave it, or sell the poles in the round for hop poles or fencing stakes, and commonly use the cloven wood for 'pale and wire' fencing: that useful, flexible and easily movable fencing used for so many purposes. This is made in a *walk*, generally by ladies, working machines which move slowly along as the individual pales are fed by hand into the machine and twisted into the horizontal wires.

Elm, alas now being slaughtered by Dutch Elm Disease, is probably a native of Britain (i.e. it was not brought here by man), although early writers thought it an alien. It is a tree of the lowlands and of heavy, good land. It is predominantly a hedgerow tree. The most important characteristic of elm wood from the point of view of the countryman is that it will not split. You cannot cleave it—and it will not cleave itself. It is very hard, not at all straight-grained, durable in the weather, and when under water all the time, but not when in contact with the ground. It is the only British wood really suitable for wheel hubs (because it does not split); it was, and is, used frequently for ships' keels (because of its durability immersed in water), for piling under water, for wedges and chocks, wheelbarrows and partitions in stables (because it will not split when bashed or kicked), pulley-blocks: anything that requires a wood that will not split. The last contact that the countryman has with wood is generally with elm, for of it his coffin is made.

The *Hawthorn* is a tree that almost every countryman comes in contact with, often painfully as it has very sharp prickles. But they say wounds made by Hawthorn prickles do not fester while those made by Blackthorn (Sloe) do! Another name for the Hawthorn is

laid hedge

the May. It is the most important of the *hedge* trees, thousands of miles of it having been planted during the Enclosures to form quickthorn hedges. If *laid* every so many years, such a hedge will last for ever and remain quite stockproof. The art of laying a hedge is to cut selected stems half through and bend them over and intertwine them with other stems. Half cut thus they do not die but continue to grow and send up shoots which form a thick hedge. Cut stakes may be driven down through the hedge at intervals to hold the bent-over stems, and the tops of these are woven, together with *ethering*—a braiding, or weaving, of thin rods, generally hazel rods. By the time the stakes and ethering has rotted the hedge has grown into itself well enough not to need them.

hazel coppice

Hazel used to be extensively coppiced, and cut for its pliable and strong slender branches. These made woven hurdles, and were once (before wire) a most important fencing material: being used to protect a young quickthorn hedge from stock before it was big enough to protect itself, and also used for movable sheep hurdles. It was, and is, also extensively used for baskets, and for *brortches*—the pegs and horizontals used by thatchers to hold their 'reed' down. Barrel hoops were often hazel: it was, and is, used for any purpose for which tough, whippy, flexible rods or bands are necessary. Life for the true countryman would be hard to imagine without the Hazel tree.

Sycamore can be, and is, used for anything the Beech is used for, and as it grows freely where the Beech does *not* grow (i.e. in the west and north, and highland Britain generally—the Beech grows in the south-east and is practically confined to calcareous soil, such as the Chalk and Oolite) it comes in very handy! It is used for turning and for carving. Most of the Welsh love-spoons, cawl (soup) bowls and other carved 'treen' ware in Wales and the north of England are made of Sycamore. It is a soft, white, clean-looking wood, ideal for such purposes.

Oak, unquestionably the king of English trees, provides (in its heart-wood only—the lighter-coloured sap wood is not much good) the finest timber if not in the world then certainly in the British Isles. When kept dry it seems practically everlasting, it is immensely strong and seems to get stronger the older it gets, and is very hard indeed. It is splendid for furniture (being very beautiful), makes the spokes of wooden wheels (for only oak will take the tremendous bashing that spokes get carrying a heavy load over a rough road), the timbers of ships, the planking too if the owner can afford it and the structural timber of buildings. Oak cleaves well, and cloven oak is stronger than sawn of course. The oak that grows predominantly in England is the Pedunculate Oak, the species that grows in Wales and Scotland mostly the Sessile. Oak survives in rough, windy, acid and infertile places, but to grow at its best, either as wide-spreading park trees or as tall straight timber in plantations, it needs the best of soil and conditions. Such good land is at a premium now for farming, but it will be a sad day for England if men no longer set aside some good land, each year, for the planting of good oak for the use of future generations.

The *Willow* is widespread all over Britain, being the most persist-ent of trees. It is the basket-maker's standby, makes hurdles, and any other woven or plaited objects. It is often used by thatchers for thatching-rods or brortches instead of Hazel, and in fact it is used for many of the purposes for which Hazel is suitable. It is very easy to plant—you just stick a branch into the ground and it grows. It is, though, very difficult to get rid of. Large *osier beds* are planted and tended in marshy places in Somerset and East Anglia, for the pro-duction of rods for basket-making. Pollarded willows are common in the eastern counties.

Walnut is, alas, hardly ever planted now, though extensively so in the past. It takes three hundred years to grow to maturity, and apparently our present landowners think this is too long to wait for a harvest. Fortunately our ancestors did not think so. It was protected by law during the Napoleonic wars for use only for gun-stocks. It is one of the most beautiful woods in existence, and lucky is the owner of walnut furniture or panelling.

Chapter 11

Transport and Travel in the Countryside

As is well known early man in Britain established trackways along such well-drained and forest-free ridges as the Icknield Way along a slope of the Chilterns, the 'Jurassic Way' along the whole length of the Oolitic Limestone outcrop from Lincoln to the coast in Dorset, the Pilgrim's Way along the North Downs, the Preseli Way along the ridge of the Preseli range—a road that connected southern England (not England then of course) with the seaports that served Ireland. Irish gold came eastward along this road—and probably flint and stone implements went westward. Theories about 'Old Straight Tracks' I feel are very suspect: I believe you can find the real equivalent of Stone Age, Bronze Age, and Iron Age tracks in such places as the forested parts of Central Africa today. Such tracks are seldom straight, and their course has been decided by physical features. They avoid swamps when they can, avoid very steep gradients, cling to long ridge-backs where possible (in many mountainous forested areas the ridges are always easy going, while the flanks of the hills, or valleys, are very difficult; many of us found this out in the Chin Hills of Burma during the last war).

The Romans built their famous network of roads, cutting as straight as they could through the country in their rather unimaginative way. Their roads may be compared to the modern motorway system in that the layout takes no account of local needs or peculiarities. The Roman roads, like the later railways and even later motorways, were built for the needs of the central government—not local

187

farmers or villagers. They don't *look* as if they fit into, or are part of, the countryside. They stride over it and ignore it.

The Anglo-Saxons and the medieval English didn't seem to bother much about roads at all. They travelled on foot or on horseback, and transported things on pack-horses. Short roads were made between one medieval manor and the next, and often these would be joined together so as to form some sort of a cross-country route, often zig-zagging wildly to avoid cutting across people's fields. We enjoy the legacy of this now in what Chesterton described in a poem beginning 'The rolling English drunkard made the rolling English road'. No doubt he did, and has used it ever since.

The enclosures of the eighteenth and nineteenth centuries caused a lot of new country roads to be built, linking up the newly formed farm homesteads with the village. The enclosures made farmers leave the compact villages and spread out over their land. Macadam, an eighteenth-century engineer, revolutionized road-making by the simple and one would have thought pretty obvious discovery that it was no good just dumping larger stones into the mud and calling it a road, but that the stones should be small and carefully graded. The stones on the surface should in all cases be small. His method was adapted all over Britain, and hundreds of vagrants and other poor people were employed breaking up stone with hammers to surface roads. Thomas Telford improved on Macadam's methods and drove great national throughways through the country, such as the great road from London to Holyhead. The establishment of stage coach services occurred at this time. The arrival of the motor car caused roads to be surfaced with tarmac (tar poured on a Macadam surface) and this process was speeded up in Wales and the West of England by the whole-milk trade that sprung up in the first half of this century, with the necessity for getting the milk lorry to every remote farmhouse once a day.

But land transport was very much a secondary thing until the invention of the railways. True there were huge broad-wheeled wagons which traversed the countryside from Tudor times onwards, and the stage coaches shortened distances for wealthier passengers in the eighteenth century enormously, the drivers picking up fresh horses every twenty miles or so and therefore being able to drive all day at a gallop. Perhaps the greatest land transporters of all were the cattle-drovers, who operated from early medieval times to the coming of the railways, driving great herds of cattle from such places as Wales and Scotland to Smithfield in London, or to graziers on the fine fattening pastures of Leicestershire, the Norfolk Broadlands, the

wagon from Montgomeryshire, Wales

Fens, and other places. These men took months over their journeys, travelling slowly to let the cattle graze on the way, so that they actually increased in weight.

A bizarre traffic was that of great droves of turkeys, which left Norfolk farms before Christmas, and walked the hundred miles up to London to arrive in time for the festival.

But by far the greater part of heavy traffic was on water, and this obtained right up to the building of the railways and in fact long after in a modified way. It was the tarmac road and the motor lorry that finally knocked water transport out.

Coastal and river transport is very ancient in these islands, and it is notable that nearly all our towns and ancient centres of population are on navigable water. Wherever we find large buildings of stone in stoneless areas (such as the magnificent churches and cathedrals of East Anglia for example) we can be sure that these buildings are not very far from navigable water, for there would have been no other practicable way of getting the stone to them. Thus medieval stone buildings in East Anglia are either built of Oolite limestone from Barnack, in Northamptonshire, brought down the Nene and then by sea and up some river, or of similar limestone brought by sea from Caen in Normandy. It would have been cheaper to bring building stone all the way from Caen to Norwich, say, by water, than to have carried it ten miles overland.

In the seventeenth century serious attempts were made to improve the navigability of rivers by flash weirs and other items. A flash weir was a wooden barrier which could be opened, built across a river. If it was closed it would hold up the water above it and increase the depth of the river for maybe a mile or two, whereby barges could get up or down with heavier lading. When the barge reached the flash weir the latter was allowed to be pushed open by the current, the barge would either shoot through on the flush of water if going downhill, or be hauled up against it by brute force if going upstream, and the weir then closed again.

It is said that Leonardo da Vinci was the first European to dream up the pound-lock, but probably the Chinese used it centuries before his time. This is two water-gates, one above the other in a stream,

Bratch locks

with sluices in them that can be opened and closed. A voyager going uphill empties the pound between the two gates, puts his vessel in it, closes the bottom gate and its sluices, opens the sluices of the top gate to allow water to run in from above, thus raising his vessel to the level of the water in the 'pound' above, then, when he 'has a level', he opens the top gate and takes the vessel through. Going downhill

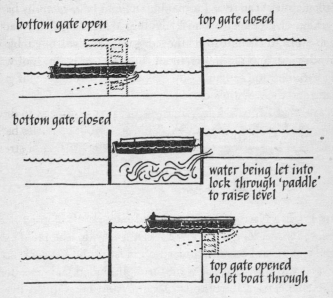

Boat using a lock to go uphill

he simply reverses this procedure. The invention of this, the true lock, enabled boats and barges to be taken high up into hills or even mountains.

The astonishing canal boom of the eighteenth and early nineteenth centuries was the result. Companies were formed all over England, in one or two places in Wales, and also in Scotland, but England, being fairly level and ripe for industrialization, had by far the most. And into being came the astonishing narrow canal system— one of the wonders of the world. Engineers such as James Brindley, and later Thomas Telford, designed canals that straggled all over England. The Humber was linked to the Mersey, Thames and Severn, every big coalfield was tapped by canals and every major centre of industry. In fact it would be true to say that there could be no centre of industry without a canal, for there was no other method of transporting, economically, the goods. For example the pottery region around Stoke-on-Trent could never flourish while the ware had to be transported away on the backs of pack-horses. When Brindley drove his great Trent and Mersey Canal through Stoke such pioneers as Wedgwood were able to build huge factories, getting their china clay from Cornwall, by ship to Runcorn, then up the canal to Stoke, their flint-stone the same way, and sending their ware to the coast by canal for shipment all over the world, or sending it by canal all the way to London.

narrow boat

The English Narrow Boat developed into a craft of great beauty. Some seventy feet long but a mere seven feet wide, she fitted exactly into the locks that became standard on most of the network, so that little water was wasted as she went through. Pulled by horse, donkey or mule, she carried thirty tons of cargo, and her captain lived on board, in a tiny cabin aft, generally with a wife and large family of children. Where they all slept is still a mystery. These people—the boat people—formed a race apart, travelling, many of them, all over England, taking their floating home with them, marrying only 'on the Cut' (i.e. other canal people—'the Cut' was their word for the canal), despising people 'off the Land'; they were hard drinkers, hard workers, some of them apt to settle arguments with a blow from their 'lock keys'—heavy iron windlasses every boatman carried in a special pocket in his trousers for winding up the sluices on the lock-gates. There are fifty-six locks between the sea and the summit of the Leeds Liverpool Canal, which is just over five hundred feet above sea-level. Going up all those locks was gruelling work, for speed was essential to make a living. Incidentally the Leeds and Liverpool is one canal that is not a narrow canal: the locks are fourteen feet wide. The

Leeds Liverpool boats are called Short Boats for they are shorter than the narrow boats. Boats should never be called barges incidentally—a barge is over fifteen feet wide, and canal boatmen should never be called 'bargees'—they are boatmen. They took great pride in their craft, and painted them bright colours, often with distinctive designs depicting roses and castles. Their water-cans, dip-cans, stools and other articles were similarly painted, and their tiny cabins were hung about with lace-edge plates and other ornamental objects. The

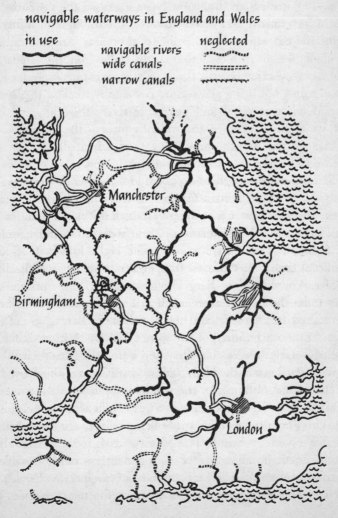

navigable waterways in England and Wales

in use   neglected

navigable rivers
wide canals
narrow canals

brass chimneys of their cabins and their horses' brass-work were brightly polished. The men wore special very flashy clothes, including broad ornamental belts, and the women distinctive dresses with poke bonnets.

The diesel engine came and did away with the horses, and the custom came to work two boats: a motor boat and a butty-boat which was towed astern. The Grand Union Canal was built to take two narrow boats alongside in its locks and this caused the two-boat system. The wash from the motor boats damaged the towpaths and the bank revetments and silted up many canals, thus lowering the draught and consequently the lading of the boats. And the railways came along, fought ruthlessly to steal the traffic from the canals, and finally in many cases bought the canals up and purposely let them fall into ruin—not being allowed by law simply to close them. Two thousand miles of canal and navigable river, though, have been saved, we hope for ever, by the valiant efforts of the Inland Waterways Association, and are now being used principally for pleasure traffic, and a holiday on the canals is delightful too.

Good and highly specialized coastal and river craft were evolved around the coasts of Britain for various carrying trades. The most famous was the East Coast Barge, sometimes called London, or Thames, Barge, although many of them were built and based far from London. There were at one time eight hundred of these magnificent craft. They carried from eighty to six or seven hundred tons of cargo: the 'River Barges' mostly carried one hundred and twenty tons: the larger barges, such as *Cambria* and *Will Everard*, two hundred and seventy, and the big 'Boomie Barges' and Ketch Barges—up to six hundred. They were all ('River Barges' included) sea-going vessels: the reason why they were called barges was that they were flat-bottomed. Their sailing qualities were improved, in spite of their flat bottoms, by the device of *leeboards*—large wooden fins that hang down on each side of a vessel and act as a keel to stop her making *leeway*—in other words being driven sideways through the water by a side wind. The 'Spritty' barges were marvels of ingenuity in their sailing rig: a man and a boy being capable of navigating two hundred and seventy tons of cargo across the sea, up rivers and mud-creeks, under low bridges (the mast lowered) and wherever it was needed. They were probably the most beautiful, and efficient, sailing craft ever developed. Alas, they trade no more, excepting a couple of dozen that lie in the Blackwater or up the Medway, and act as houseboats, pleasure-boats, or take paying passengers.

a model of a
Humber keel

It has been said, with some justification, that it was the spritsail barge that made London possible, for only this cheap and marvellously effective form of transport could have carried the huge quantities of food for people and horses to the capital, and taken the enormous quantities of horse manure away again, back to the farms where it could do some good, this made necessary by a city which moved entirely by horses. The last barge to trade commercially, and quite unsubsidized, was the *Cambria*, Captain 'Bob' Roberts, and she is now a floating museum at Rochester, Kent, and seems to me to be one of the most beautiful works of man in England. I have had the honour of sailing aboard her, many times, as Third Hand.

Other vanished coasting and river craft are the Wherries of the Norfolk Broads: boats rather than barges, and ideally suited for carrying cargoes along the narrow rivers of Broadland. They had enormously thick masts which could be lowered and raised by their forestays and which were counterbalanced by lead weights at the butt so that 'a child could raise them with one finger'. They set one huge black-tanned sail held up by a very long gaff and no foresail. Such was the shape of their hulls and cut of their rig that they could sail very close to the wind, turn to windward up the narrowest of channels,

and they had a power of shouldering themselves along a lee bank
when sailing close to the wind such as no other vessel ever had. One
man could sail them, dropping the mast to shoot bridges and raising
it before the boat lost way, and many of them had false keels, bolted
on to their real ones, which could be dropped when the wherry had
to go up a shallow river and bolted on again when she returned to
deep water. They were superbly evolved for their task in very exacting waters. They carried from thirty to forty tons. There is one kept

Norfolk wherries - under power and sail

as a show-piece: the *Albion*, by the Norfolk Wherry Trust, and there
are several cut-down wherries in existence used as motor boats or
dumb barges.

Moving north to the Humber we get the Humber Keel, again a
craft perfectly suited for her job and waters. She had to be fairly
short—to get through the locks on the Sheffield Canal—and beamy
to fit these same locks with the maximum of cargo. She carried about
eighty tons, carried lee-boards like an East Coast Barge, was not
quite flat-bottomed in that she had a keel and rounded chines
(rounded chines were safer when a barge was caught beam-on on
one of the *racks*—sand or gravel banks—of the Trent or Humber,
where a hard-chined barge might have been turned over by the
seven- or eight-knot tide) and she set a square sail on one lowering
mast, with often another square sail over the top of it. All sheets,
halliards and braces, and the mast-raising forestay, were led to windlasses and the vessel could be managed by one man. There are
several old keels still working, although all with engines now and

none with sailing gear. They centre on Hull and trade to Nottingham, York, and other places. An attempt was made to preserve one working keel in sail by the Humber Keel Trust, but the people of the Humber, apparently, did not have the same local pride as the Norfolk men and the project failed for lack of support.

The Tyne Keel was another local river carrier ('Weel may the keel row' is a song about this vessel) and was used for carrying coal from the mines to ships. The Mersey Flat was the Mersey version—a fast and powerful sailing vessel, cutter-rigged, more of a sea-going vessel perhaps than the Humber Keel. The Severn had her *Trows*: strange, heavy, beamy, medieval-looking boats, some setting square sails on two masts, some fore-and-aft in rig, with high aftercastles. They worked the fierce tidal reaches of the Severn Estuary, riding out the famous Severn Bore, and it is said that their captains used to fasten the anchor chain with a stout twig of wood when they lay at anchor waiting for a change of tide. When the tide did turn, and the vessel swung to it, the strain would break the twig and the noise of cable running out would rouse the crew from their slumbers, and they would promptly get up and weigh anchor. Barges pulled by men called *bow-hauliers* would ply up the non-tidal Severn as far as Shrewsbury, and also up the Stratford Avon. It is said that the hauliers were rough men, and that men would lock up their chickens —and their daughters—when they heard the sound of the hauliers' voices singing as they hove on the ropes. The Solent, and the Rother system, the Fal, the Tamar, all had their distinctive barges or boats. The Fens had the famous Fen Lighters, which worked in trains of four or five, the whole train pulled by a horse. They had to be short, to get through the medieval locks of the Fen Waterways and therefore went in trains so that one horse could pull a big enough load. They were steered round corners by a strange arrangement of *sprits* and *fest ropes*. The sprit of each overhung the stern of the next, and two tackles, called fest ropes, went from the end of the sprit to each quarter of the barge in front. A man would lengthen one tackle and haul in on the other to make the train go round a sharp corner—one man could do it by racing aft from the foremost lighter to the next one, and so on. When the horse had to cross a river the horse merely stepped aboard a special place on a lighter, and he rode thus also when there was a fair wind and the foremost lighter could set a squaresail, or when the train was in tidal waters and could drive along on the tide. The Fen Lightermen, like all these inland sailors, were roistering fellows. Vic Jackson, the last survivor of them, lives at Stanground Creek near Peterborough, and can tell many stories of stirring times. It is recounted of him that, when his train of lighters had gone over to steam tug, he would put one sack for one individual farm on each of five lighters (assuming he had to deliver five sacks) and would jump from lighter to lighter, carrying a two-hundred-weight sack ashore from each one and placing it in the farmer's cart, without the tug having to slacken speed. These Lighters were once

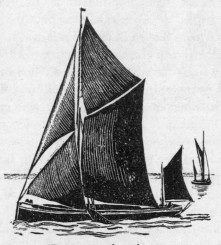

Thames sailing barge

the main transport system of the whole of the Great Level, linking King's Lynn with Boston, both with Ely and Peterborough, trading to Cambridge, up the Great Ouse to Bedford, the Nene to Northampton, and taking in nearly all the farms and villages of Fenland, along the intricate system of waterways and drains. Now none are left, save some rotting hulks at Wansford, on the Nene. Vic Jackson has a good model of one, though.

The four great estuaries of the Thames, Humber, Mersey and Severn, and the inlet of the Wash, were connected, as we have seen, to each other and to every major industrial area of England, by canals, so that before the railways came the country had a marvellous system of heavy transport. Now all that is left of inland water transport are motor barges connecting the various parts of London River with Kentish and Essex and Suffolk ports, motor keels and British Waterways motorized barges plying the Trent, Humber, and Yorkshire Ouse, the famous 'Tom Puddings' which are steel boxes hauled

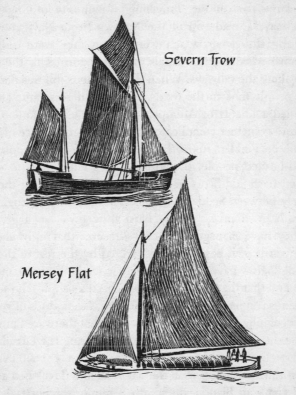

Severn Trow

Mersey Flat

or pushed in trains by tugs, carrying coal from the mines to Goole to be shot into ships, a fleet of motorized Flats on the Mersey still, and barges carrying mostly timber going up-Severn as far as Stourport. There are river tankers on many of these systems still, but these will inevitably be knocked out in due course by pipelines. Coasting vessels are beyond the scope of this book. What the future has in store for water transport—no man can tell. Certainly, every rise in the price of oil brings the time when a man and a horse working a boat carrying thirty tons of cargo, albeit slowly, approaches, by ever so little, the cost-effectiveness of a thirty-ton lorry.

An important element in the country life of the British Isles is the Travelling People.

Travellers, as they like to call themselves (not to be confused with commercial travellers!) are people of diverse origins, racial and otherwise. A large part of the Travelling community of England, for example, may be made up of the Navvies (from Navigators—they came to dig the canals which were, when they were dug, called Navigations) who dug the canals and then turned to the colossal task of making the railways. When the enormous job was done many of these people took to the roads, and their descendants are sometimes called Didikois or Mumpers or—by the ignorant—Gypsies. The picture is further complicated by the mysterious race of Tinkers in Ireland, or Tinklers in Scotland, who are the same people. These are a red-headed people, thought by some authorities to antedate the settled Irish and Scots in their respective countries; they move very freely between Scotland and Ireland, and invade England and Wales in large numbers. They have their own language, Shelta, which they have managed to keep so secret that only about five hundred words of it have been discovered by the rest of the world. Some philologists have suggested that it might be connected with Lappish, and that the Tinkers may have been a people who settled in various lands connected by the Northern Seas thousands of years ago. A further complication of their language is that there are Latin words in it, brought in by Irish monks displaced during the Dissolution of the Monasteries, and forced to take to the roads as common vagrants. They naturally joined up with the Tinkers, and developed a kind of Thieves' Cant, or Slang, which was a mix-up of Shelta and dog-Latin.

But the backbone of the Travelling population of England itself, and Wales too, is the true Gypsy, or Romany. Gypsies were first reported in literature in the *Shah Nama*, or Persian Book of Kings, as having crossed from Hind in the thirteenth century, having been expelled by the ruler of that land, and having been welcomed by the Shah of Persia as travelling musicians. Thereafter the history of their gradual spread into the Middle East and Europe can be traced by historical records. They invented some elaborate story of being the Kings of Lower Egypt, expelled for the part of one of them who forged the nails of the Cross, and therefore condemned to wander for a thousand years. They forged letters purporting to be from the Pope to this effect, and were therefore welcomed in many European countries, but their welcome commonly turned sour and laws were passed to drive them out: in places they were hunted like animals, in Hungary the whole Gypsy race was enslaved.

They arrived in Britain in Edinburgh in the sixteenth century, and soon moved to cover the whole country. They were at that time horsemen, horse-traders, tinkers (not racially but professionally—they mended and made tin vessels), metal-workers, fortune-tellers, spell-casters, basket-makers and peg-makers. They lived in tents which they carried on pack-horses. They spoke their own language, which had a firm basis of Hindi, or Hindustani, with accretions picked up along the route from India. Philologists can trace the route of any particular tribe of Gypsies in Europe (where they retain

bow-topped Romany caravans

their distinct tribes) by studying the brand of Romany which they talk. They have lost all but a vestige of their language in Britain today, but there are still a very few who can speak the pure, inflected Romany without much admixture of English or Welsh words, and nearly every Gypsy knows enough nouns and verbs to be able to intersperse sufficient with his English to make his language unintelligible to the *Gorgio*, or Gentile.

They moved into horse-drawn caravans, or *Vardos*, at the end of the nineteenth century, but now live either in houses, and try to merge as much as they can with the native population, or in trailer-caravans, pulled behind lorries. They have always adapted to meet new conditions, and now their commonest trade is scrap-dealing, and without them the scrap trade of England would collapse and our land would be soon covered with junk. They do a very valuable service with their scrap-collecting, cleaning the country up and re-cycling what would otherwise be waste material. The very nature of this trade, though, makes their own camp sites appear untidy, and arouses the righteous wrath of the oh-so-tidy *Gorgio*, who doesn't realize that if it weren't for the Gypsy he would be swamped in his own rubbish. Gypsies, when you get to know them, are the best company in the world: lively, intelligent, restless and vivacious, with enormous verve and zest for living. They have permeated country society much more than people generally know. Most villages have people with Gypsy blood in them, and the true countryman, no matter how he may fear and hate the travelling Gypsy or indeed any outsider, has a sneaking regard for these people of the roads, who appear to come and go as they please, with their fine lurcher dogs, their horses, their scrap-lorries and flash trailers, their boozing and their singing and their fighting, and their apparent stance of being outside our laws.

People commonly say: 'There are no real Gypsies left nowadays.' There are, in fact, more than ever. They just don't show up as much as they used to, that is all. Determined efforts are now being made to settle them, and in fact to discourage them from existing. But some-how one feels that the Gypsy will always survive.

Chapter 12

Not by Bread Alone

The countryman has always been a religious man, and he still is, although nowadays he very probably does not go to church (the big farmers' wives do, and the rusticated town gentry who are trying to 'get in'), and he may well tell you that he is an atheist or an agnostic. But you cannot work with living creatures under the sky, and in all weathers, without developing a sense of awe, and a sense of awe is all that religion is. The landsman sees the sun come swinging up into the heavens in the mornings, and sink beneath the western skyline at night, and when he goes out at night—to work, or visit, or poach—the bright stars sing above him in the heavens, and he is made aware all the time that he lives on a planet that hurtles through space steered and governed by laws that nobody yet understands. Therefore he has a sense of awe, that may be missing, or at least muted, in people who see the stars dimmed by neon lighting, and seldom see the sunrise because they are in bed, or the sunset because it is obscured by high buildings and have little time to reflect by the urgent necessity to read at least two newspapers a day besides looking at the television.

During the Middle Ages there was just no problem about religion. If we wish to experience what religious feeling among country people was like at that time we must go to India. Join in a pilgrimage to Badrachalam (at the period when the waters of the Ganges are thought to be running down the Godavari), or Ramaswaram, or Madura, and you will have a very good idea of what it was like to be a pilgrim to Canterbury, or Walsingham, or Compostela, in the fourteenth century. Religion pervaded life and life religion and no distinction was made between the two. The plough was blessed in church and thereafter dragged around the village from house to house in procession—and each householder had to give largesse to the instrument and the men whom they still knew, in those days, kept them alive. Holidays were holydays and there was no distinction between the two words: men invoked the name of God constantly in their everyday lives, as men do in India today. A reading of *The Vision of Piers Plowman* quickly convinces one of the all-pervading nature of belief in God in those times: everything that happened was put down to the workings of the Divinity.

Then came the Renaissance, and Doubt, but among country people it took a long time for Doubt to creep in—in fact there are *still* old country people who say things like: 'If God had meant us to fly he'd ha' given us wings!' And they mean what they say.

Puritanism, in the seventeenth century, practically brought to an end the celebrations of the countryside. The new religion of industriousness and sobriety had no time for Plough Sundays and Barley Saturdays and May Day junketings and Old New Years and Well-Dressing ceremonies and all the rest of it. The workers were there to work and their employers to make money. And the new industry and inventiveness that followed the liberation of the Renaissance and the iconoclasm of Puritanism benefited not one jot the labouring countryman but brought new heights of comfort and luxury to the great and wealthy.

There was a brief revival of Merry England in the Restoration and the reign of Charles II; then, in the eighteenth century, religion for most country people meant weekly attendance at a parish church from which all spark of real religious zeal or awe had departed. The parson owed his position to 'preferment' from some wealthy patron of the church, probably because he was the younger son of some wealthy friend. Poor people went to church because they had to (they would quickly lose their jobs and their cottages if they stayed away), tenant farmers went for the same reason, the squires went to 'set an example to the lower orders'. Religion was one great yawn, and whatever religious feelings men had were felt outside the walls of the parish church.

Then came Wesley and the other revivalists. Wesley was a Church of England parson, and tried to reform the Church from within—but the movement quickly burst its bonds and broke right away from the dead hand of the Establishment. It swept the British Isles (excepting the Catholic parts of Ireland) like a forest fire and nothing could put it out. Tenants defied their landlords and broke from the Church and went to Chapel, labourers cheerfully went to gaol, or were turned out of their jobs and cottages, people met in secret in 'meeting houses', or in public in huge outdoor gatherings at which religious fervour, often crossing the border into hysteria, was whipped up. The Establishment was powerless to stop it. The law had to be changed—and changed again—to accommodate it, since to try to suppress it would have brought about revolution. Chapels sprung up in every village in England and Wales. Suppression went on as far as it could: right into this century there were landlords who would not let a farm to a Nonconformist tenant, and farmers who would not employ a 'Chapel' labourer. But in the end the squires had to yield to the inevitable. If they were to hold the reigns of power and privilege in the countryside it was *not* to be through the Established Church.

A few farm labourers and family retainers still clung to the old religion, and still do. But to attend a service in a Baptist Chapel today, and to attend one the following Sunday in the parish Church, is to find a great contrast. The Chapel is full—the Church is three-quarters empty. When people sing in Chapel they sing with loud voices and with fervour. Singing in Church is a very muted and well-bred affair—the women (who make up three-quarters at least of the congregation) warbling in scarcely hearable, carefully modulated voices, the men just grunting in an embarrassed and discordant way. In England the Chapel singing, though enthusiastic, may lack quality: in Welsh chapels you will hear some of the most sophisticated choral singing in the world, for the ability to harmonize and a good voice seem to be born in every Welsh child.

Sadly we have no idea of the *folk song* of the Middle Ages: nearly all trace of it was suppressed, first by seventeenth-century Puritanism, then by Victorian kill-joyism. But folk songs from Tudor times onwards incredibly linger on as part of the oral culture of that illiterate race, the Gypsies (as they gain literacy they lose this culture automatically), in the memories of a few old people, and now more and more in the written collections of folk-lore enthusiasts, like the Hammond brothers, who themselves collected at least forty songs (which no doubt would otherwise have died) in the early years of this century.

It is not possible to transcribe perfectly the music of folk songs, for the true folk singer did not read music, nor did he ever stick to 'true pitch' unless he wanted to. There is still a handful of old men and women who sing in the real old folk tradition, and a smaller handful of young people who were taught, from the cradle, by such old people, but it is a dying rearguard. The juke box and the contempt of thoughtless youth have finished the job that the Victorian 'drawing-room ballad', Methodist hymn-singing, and eighteenth-century jingoistic songs, failed to complete.

But you still hear some of the old songs, sung as they were meant to be sung by people who have learnt them from their parents, if you know where to look:

It was pleasant and delightful on a mid-summer's morn
And the green fields and the meadows they were buried in corn
And the blackbirds and the thrushes
Sang on every green tree
And the larks they sang melodious at the dawning of the day!

Such lyricism—as good of its kind as any poetry that has ever been written (but that was *not* written) still lingers on in some Suffolk pubs sung almost by stealth when for some reason the juke box is temporarily silent.

Much existing folk song is the product of the eighteenth century when Britain ruled the waves—but ruled them at the expense of the lives and loves of many poor country people, as this and hundreds of other songs of the period testify:

Said a sailor to his true love I am bound far away
For our topsails they are hoisted and our anchor's a'weigh
And our good ship lies waiting
For the next flowing tide
And if ever I come home again I will make you my bride!

Now the ring from her finger she instantly drew
Saying take this dearest William and my heart with it too!
And while he was embracing her
Tears from her eyes fell
Saying, May I go along with you?
Oh no my love—farewell!

It was farewell in many of these songs. And often farewell with
the hint that the beloved was never to return again.

For I'm bound to India for seven long year
Drinking wine and strong whisky, Love, instead of good beer,
But if ever I come home again it'll be in some Spring
And we'll both sit down together Love to hear the nightingales
sing.

The songs that survive to us tell of roving, love, courtship (always
tender and sweet but often ending with the sad betrayal of the lass),
marriage (generally sour) and plain bawdy. Consider this song collected by the good Mr Gardiner in 1907 from the respectable Mrs
Goodyear of Axford, Basingstoke, Hants:

There was an old woman lived under a hill
With my rowdy-dow-dow, with my rowdy-dow-day
And if she isn't gone she lives there still
Ah-ha-ha was it so was it so?
A jolly dragoon came riding by
He called for a pot because he was dry
He drinked him up and called for another
He kissed the daughter fair, likewise the old mother
The night came on, the day being spent
They both went to bed with the mother's consent
Oh! what is this so stiff and warm
'Tis only my nag—he'll do you no harm
But what is this? 'Tis a little well
Where your fine nag may drink his fill
But what if my bonny nag should chance to fall in?
He must hang on the grass that grows round the brim
But what if the grass should prove to be rotten?
He must bob up and down 'til he comes to the bottom.

English folk song tended to be radical, and to speak for the under-dog. It was never political—it knew nothing of revolution or reform or social consciousness. It accepted the *status quo* as something quite immutable—and then sang of the sufferings and vicissitudes of people who lived under it. There are many songs of poaching, of crime (although these were chiefly urban), of smuggling, and of servants and underlings getting their own back, in their own, quite unpolitical, way, on their masters:

> Come all ye frollicking fellows!
> I'd have ye listen to me
> I'd have ye come up with your rat-tat-tat-tat
> When ye're master's out of the way
> > When your master goes a'roving
> > To view the fields so gay
> Then I'd have ye come up with your rat-tat-tat-tat
> Be it either by night or day!
> Be it either by night or day!

This exhortation was addressed by a 'gentleman's servant' to his colleagues after describing how he had 'minded his master's business' to the extent of taking that worthy's place in bed with his wife. There are many such songs.

But through all the English countryman's folk songs runs a strong current of lyricism—of a real love and passion for the countryside, and country life, and the beautiful things of nature and of the farm:

> As I was a'walking one morning in the Spring
> I heard a fair damsel so sweetly she did sing
> And as we were a'walking she unto me did say
> There's no life like the ploughboy's all in the month of May.

> > The lark in the morning she rises from her nest
> > And mounts in the bright air with the dew all on her breast
> > And with the pretty ploughboy she'll whistle and she'll sing
> > And at night she'll return to her nest once again!

But the fair damsel in this story, like the one in so many others, does not escape unchanged.

Her mammy asked the reason why she thickened
round the waist ...

It was no wonder, perhaps, that Church and Chapel alike frowned on English vernacular folk song.

Folk *dance* lingered on too, preserved in pubs in remote villages (pubs like the Blaxhall 'Ship' in Suffolk, where the juke box was not installed until the 1960s) and also, like song and other traditions, by the Gypsies. Under many a bang-up-to-date chrome-plated trailer living-van you will find an old piece of board and may wonder what this is for. It is to be hauled out in the evening, and flung down by the *yog* or camp fire, for 'Auntie so-and-so' or 'Uncle so-and-so' to do the old English *step dance* on. The step dance bears no relation to the effete 'tap-dancing' that came from Hollywood in the nineteen-twenties and -thirties: it is a fine, vigorous, very restrained and disciplined and yet enormously virile form of dancing and as English as Yorkshire pudding. When a man or a woman gets up to 'step' to the lively music of melodies, mouth organ or fiddle the onlookers will cry '*Cut* in there! *Cut* in there!' to someone of the opposite sex who only needs a little of such urging to leap up, face the dancer, and, with arms held stiffly down at his or her sides—holding head up and gazing straight ahead, dancing always on the same spot—start moving the feet at a speed and with a rhythm that defines imitation by anyone who has not learnt the art as a child. The current guitar-playing folk revivalists (and more strength to them!) should learn this art of step-dancing, if they can, but it is not easy.

Morris dancing never quite died, and is now being revived through-out the land. First attempts to revive it—under the auspices of the daughters of the vicarage mostly—gave it a certain precious con-notation, but this is vanishing, and if you go to Bampton in Oxford-shire at Whitsun, for example, you will see a most masculine and lively dance—its masculinity not impaired in any way by the pretty ribands and bells and white clothes and straw hats of the dancers. At its best it is extremely skilful, extremely graceful, and very virile.

In Wales dancing was almost entirely extirpated by the great Nonconformist revival, which looked upon anything so secular and so sensual as dancing as very sinful. Even now, in any Welsh party,

you are most unlikely to see any dancing except the wrigglings of Pop
or the wishy-washy passionless exercise known as 'ballroom dancing'. There is a conscious revival though, and it can be hoped that
as new generations revise their idea of what is sinful, and as national-
ist sentiment takes a hold of the younger people, Welsh dance will
revive. It was certainly once a very rich and lively tradition. The
Welsh originally had Morris dancing, of a processional character:
indeed the idea is gaining ground that Morris was a Celtic dance
originally taken over by the English. They had, until early in the last
century, many country dances too, with names like *Dawnsio Haf* (the
summer dance), *Dawns y Fedwen* (Dance of the Birch Tree) and
Croen y Ddafad Felan (Dance of the Yellow Sheepskin). Most English
observers who wrote of Welsh dancing, at the time when it still
existed, were struck by its grace but also by its complication: as one
wrote in 1798: '. . . 'tis true there is no great variety of the figures

of them, but the few they perform are so complicated and long, that they would render an apprenticeship to them necessary in an Englishman.'

Welsh *penillion* singing is enjoying a strong revival. This is the art of singing and performing on an instrument two tunes at once, which skilfully interweave in counterpoint. The Welsh harp, too, is being revived, though the enormous cost of harps now is making this a slow process. A strange phenomenon was the survival of Welsh harp music, in an altered form, in the hands of two Gypsy families—the Roberts and the Woods—during Queen Victoria's reign. One survivor of these two families, now respectably married to a *Gorgio* or non-Gypsy of high standing, can still play the harp of her forefathers, but by the time the tradition had been handed on to her, waltzes and polkas had replaced Welsh music.

There still linger a few of the old local festivals and traditions that were not quite extirpated by various religious revivals. The widespread *horkeys*, or harvest festivals, have died out in all but a very few farms, but up until the middle of the last century they were still widely held. In south-eastern England, for example, the great gangs of mowers who mowed the corn with scythes were led by the 'Lord of the Harvest' and his 'Lady'. The 'Lady' was a man. There was much badinage and rough gaiety—but always of a strictly traditional nature. A new mower had to go through the ceremony of 'shoeing the colt'. He had to be turned upside down and have the soles of his boots hammered with a hammer—and then pay for beer all round for his elders and betters. Any stranger coming into the harvest field was greeted by the 'Holloaing of largesse'. 'Largesse—largesse!' the reapers were entitled to cry and the stranger had to give them a penny or a shilling, depending how rich he was, for beer. Elaborate ceremonials were observed on the cutting of the last sheaf (the Suffolk version is described in great detail and complete accuracy in the Reverend Cobbold's novel: *Margaret Catchpole—the Story of a Suffolk Lass*). In some areas the last sheaf was called the *neck*, and had to be cut by the reapers throwing a sickle at it from a distance. The man who was successful had the privilege of carrying it to a neighbouring farmhouse, the occupants of which had not yet finished cutting their corn. He had to do this by stealth, for if the womenfolk of the farmhouse saw him they could throw water on him and chase him away. But if he succeeded in getting the neck into their house undetected they had to feast him and there was much fun and jollity. The last sheaf, too, was traditionally made into a *corn dolly*, which was preserved until the next harvest, to harbour the Spirit of the Corn. Such customs can hardly be expected to survive the combine harvester—nor is it possible unselfconsciously to revive them. One

suspects they are gone for ever. 'Wassailing the Apple Trees' still goes on in some parts of the West Country cider areas. People go out into the cider orchards on January 17th, Old Twelfth Night, and drink cider, and pour a little on the trees, and fire shotguns into the branches and put toast and cake soaked in cider in the branches. This ensures a good crop next year.

The celebration of events in the 'Old' calendar still goes on in many parts of the British Isles. By the mid-eighteenth century it was obvious that the calendar was out of step with the actual year, and so, in 1751, Pope Gregory ordered eleven days to be dropped from the year. In 1800 another day was dropped. Many country people refused to recognize the change, and in my own valley in Wales we still celebrate *Hen Galan*, or the Old New Year, on January 12th and 13th.

Up and down the British Isles there are still very local ceremonies and observances: the New Year's Eve 'Tar Burning' at Allendale in Northumberland; Up-Helly-Aa at Lerwick in the Shetland Islands, where on the last day of January a replica Viking longship is burnt after days of feasting; the famous Furry Dance on May 8th at Helston in Cornwall and in scores of other places such relics of pagan times, or truly Christian times, are still observed. Some such customs have been self-consciously revived but a surprising number have never quite been extinguished in spite of many attempts on the part of authority to do so. It is forgotten now that, during the Commonwealth period in England, it was strictly against the law to observe Christmas in any way, either by religious observance, feasting, or staying away from work. When Christmas was allowed again, at the Restoration, it reappeared in a very watered-down and secular guise.

The country people, who were the only begetters of folk song, dance, and rural traditions, turned entirely away from them. They embraced whole-heartedly the new sophisticated electronic culture of the big cities and turned away from their own culture believing it to be inferior. But their culture was discovered by the most sophisticated of the city people—people who had the sensibility to distinguish between the real and the bogus, between good art and kitsch. And these few people have preserved rural culture and, who knows, the country people may turn to it again. Achieving a certain, rather low, degree of sophistication made them despise it. Achieving a much higher degree of sophistication may make them take to it again, and it will not be a static thing then, but will develop, as it always has developed, over the years.

> So good luck to the Ploughboy where 'ere he may be
> Who loves to have a Fair Maid to sit on his knee
> With a jug of strong ale love he'll whistle and he'll sing
> And the Ploughboy's as happy as a prince or a king!

Chapter 13

The Probable Future of Our Countryside

If we project present tendencies in British farming we will find ourselves in a land of even more enormous farms than the ones we have now (it is not fanciful to imagine, if present trends continue, whole counties under the ownership of one man or company). There will be no hedges or ditches, trees will either be in huge forests or not at all, huge machines will crawl across the landscape but no human figures will ever be seen, vast areas of the same crop will be grown. No animals or birds will be visible: domestic animals and birds will all be housed in enormous windowless buildings and wild animals and birds will have died out, having had their natural habitat destroyed.

Probably, if such trends continue, large areas of what is now called 'marginal land' will have been set aside for nature reserves, and there will be no farming in these whatever. It is into these areas that we will have to go in order to see what 'countryside' looks like, but it will not be like the countryside of our childhood, but wilderness. It will probably be full of notice boards and controlled by innumerable rules and regulations.

Many large and financially successful farmers in this country (and most of the agricultural press apparently) would welcome such developments. But there is just a chance that these people may be disappointed. For there is a counter movement going on. It is rather as if, watching the ebb tide in an estuary, you see—as you sometimes do—a counter-current, down at the mouth, with water creeping in under the outward flood just stirring the sand the other way.

Joining the Common Market has apparently pushed things much

further along the road to huge farms and 'agribusiness'. We are constantly being exhorted to 'rationalize our farming in order to compete with our fellow members of the European Economic Community'. They are much more 'efficient' than us we are told, and we will be driven out of business if we do not continue to enlarge, mechanize, and chemicalize our farms even further than we have done.

But the advocates of bigger and bigger units are meeting with unexpected resistance. An attempt to bribe farmers to get out of their farms and allow neighbouring farmers to buy them up and amalgamate them has met with an almost total lack of response. And for some ten years or so now, nearly every smallholding, or very small farm, that has been up for sale has been bought by a new sort of farmer: the sophisticated city person who wishes to get out into the country, and either farm a small piece of it for a living, or else live on it, grow at least some of his own food, and earn the rest of his living at some trade or craft. There are areas of the country today where a large proportion of the rural population is made up of such people, and there is no doubt that if more land was released for sale, and the planning restrictions eased to allow people to build houses on their own holdings, there would be a large and ever-growing exodus from the big cities into the countryside.

The price of *power* has more bearing on the pattern of agriculture than anything else. It was horse power that powered the great agricultural revolution in the late eighteenth century (aided by lavish use of manpower)—a revolution which brought the best of English farming to the highest peak of production that it ever reached. Two tons of wheat per acre were achieved on the best farms at that time with no input of fertilizers from outside the holding whatever. The present national average, with enormous inputs of imported fertilizer, is well below this. Coal-power had surprisingly little impact on farming. The steam engines were too heavy for the land, the 'steam tackles' that hauled implements backwards and forwards across the fields on ropes were far too expensive and cumbersome: the driving of threshing machines and barn machinery was the chief use to which steam was put. Throughout the age of steam the horse was still king.

Oil started taking over during the First World War, ran neck and neck with horses until the Second, and during that war the horse almost completely disappeared. Since the Second World War tractors have become more and more powerful and sophisticated, so has machinery, and battery of chemicals, both fertilizers and poisons (pesticides, fungicides and herbicides) has grown to enormous proportions. Cheap oil was the basis of it all. Efficiency of scale overrode all other kinds of efficiency, for one man with the new machinery could till a thousand acres: men were dear, oil was cheap, and so farms grew bigger and bigger.

Oil has increased in price recently in relation to other things and there have been some agonizing reappraisals. Even though the price of food has doubled, farmers are not making as much profit as they were a few years ago. Farming has always been subject to alternate booms and slumps, but entry into the Common Market seems to have accentuated this. In 1974, in accordance with Common Market policy, the British government paid a bounty to farmers to 'get out of milk'. Many milk farmers sold their cows and went into beef. Hence the next year we had the 'beef mountain', the price of beef fell away to very little and many a good farmer went bankrupt. Now many farmers are retrenching with everything: the price of cattle food and fertilizers has gone up to such a level that farmers are using less of them and cutting down on production.

A new interest has arisen in organic farming: farming without large inputs of artificial fertilizer and other chemicals. Cambridge University is currently making a study of some of the few existing organic farmers in Britain in order to see if this is not, in the end, the way out. As the price of oil rises so organic farming becomes more competitive. But organic farming needs *labour*. At present labour is very expensive (although members of the Farm Workers' Union might not think so), and this inhibits labour-intensive enterprises. But unemployment is rising in the cities and more and more city people want to get out into the countryside.

So there are signs of a reverse flow—a flow of people back to the land. This migration goes on in spite of great difficulties. Existing highly mechanized farmers are reluctant to take any more workers on: they will hang on to their high-energy-input farming for as long as they possibly can for it is now all they know. People from the cities are reluctant to become 'farm labourers'. Their forefathers fled from that to the cities. They seek their own pieces of land. A few of them have found them. Communities and communes are being formed at a rising rate. These people put up buildings, plant orchards and trees, till gardens. If they become numerous enough, and manage to break down the barriers that at present are in their way, they may change the countryside again.

There is only one thing that the countryman can feel quite sure of, and that is that the pattern of farming, and with it the character of our countryside, is not static. It has changed in the past more or less continually, and it will continue to change. It may seem that all change is brought about by the blind workings of economics. But it is true that we, the people of Britain, can bring about changes of our own free will. We get the countryside that we deserve.

Index

Turkeys, 151
Turner, Mrs Edith, 18
Turner, William, 38
Turnip, 120
  introduction of, 38

Vegetable crops, 121

Walnut, 186
Water, canals, 191
  locks, 191
  transport by, 189
Watermills, 78
Weasel, 156
Welsh dance, 210

Welsh long house, 65, 70
Wheat, 110
  diseases, 113
Wheeled plough, 100
Wherries, 195
Wildfowlers, 167
Willow, 186
Windmills, 80
Woodcock, 167
Wood pigeon, 159

Yew, 174
Young, Arthur, 40, 113

Zero-grazing, 93

MORE ABOUT PENGUINS
AND PELICANS

Penguinews, which appears every month, contains details of all the new books issued by Penguins as they are published. From time to time it is supplemented by our stocklist, which includes around 5,000 titles.

A specimen copy of *Penguinews* will be sent to you free on request. Please write to Dept EP, Penguin Books Ltd, Harmondsworth, Middlesex, for your copy.

In the U.S.A: For a complete list of books available from Penguins in the United States write to Dept CS, Penguin Books, 625 Madison Avenue, New York, New York 10022.

In Canada: For a complete list of books available from Penguins in Canada write to Penguin Books Canada Ltd, 2801 John Street, Markham, Ontario L3R 1B4.